Kahoot!
QUIZ TIME
HUMAN BODY

DK

Contents

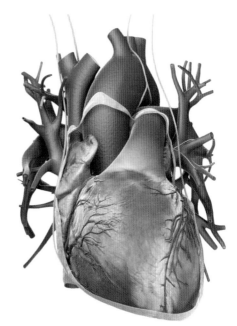

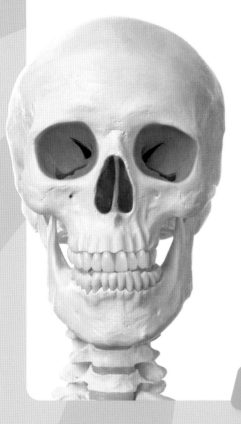

Introduction

What's the longest bone in your body? How many layers does your skin have? Can humans last for longer without food, or water? Test your knowledge of the human body in this quiz, packed with questions and facts.

You'll be quizzed on everything from the heart, to X-rays, and teeth. Celebrate the wonder of the human body and all the incredible things it can do!

Keep score

Most quizzes in this book have 10 questions each. To keep score, you'll need to record the number of correct answers each player gets after each quiz.

Keep track on a piece of paper, or even on a spreadsheet. Be sure to tally up the score for each quiz in order to crown the ultimate winner, based on who gets the highest score from all 30 quizzes. Who will grab the gold medal?

Find more quizzes!

Look for QR codes throughout the book. Scan them to find exclusive online quizzes in the same theme. You can also head over to www.kahoot.com to discover more than 100 million quizzes on loads of interesting subjects!

Find 15 QR codes like this one on the pages that follow.

Make your own

Once you've completed these quizzes, get inspired to create your own on kahoot.com!

First, plan out your questions on paper and check out our top tips to make your quiz the best it can be. When it's ready, share your quiz with friends and family.

Don't worry about who wins or if your quiz doesn't turn out exactly how you planned. The important thing is to have fun . . . but it's even more important to stay safe online. Never share any personal information with anyone online and always use the internet with a trusted adult.

Top tips

1 Do your research and always check your facts with three trusted online sources.

2 Give your quiz a fun theme and vary your questions so the quiz doesn't get repetitive.

3 Include three or four multiple choice options, plus a few true or false and picture rounds.

Skeleton

Don't be a lazy bones . . .
It's time to give this
skeleton quiz a try!

1 **What part of your skeleton protects your heart and lungs?**
- ◆ Skull
- ▲ Spine
- ● Kneecap
- ■ Rib cage

2 **The spine is made up of 26 bones, but what are they called?**
- ◆ Vertebrae
- ▲ Veins
- ● Ribs
- ■ Spinal bones

3 **Put these bones in the order they appear from top to bottom in a human skeleton:**
- ◆ Pelvis
- ▲ Skull
- ● Femur
- ■ Humerus

4 **True or false: Blood cells are produced in bone marrow.**
- ◆ True
- ▲ False

5 How many bones make up the adult skeleton?
- ◆ 56
- ▲ 106
- ● 206
- ■ 306

6 Where can you find the smallest bones in the human body?
- ◆ Finger
- ▲ Ear
- ● Nose

7 What's the longest bone in your body?
- ◆ Backbone
- ▲ Femur
- ● Collar bone

Did you know?
Around 650 of your muscles are wrapped around your bones to help you move.

8 True or false: More than half of all your bones are in your hands and feet.
- ◆ True
- ▲ False

9 Which one of these is not a type of joint found in the skeleton?
- ◆ Slider
- ▲ Gliding
- ● Ball and socket
- ■ Pivot

Scan the QR code for a Kahoot! about skeletons.

Turn to page 8 for the answers!

10 True or false: Human bones are completely solid structures.
- ◆ True
- ▲ False

Skeleton Answers

1 **What part of your skeleton protects your heart and lungs?**

■ Rib cage

Bones that make up the rib cage have an important job to do, protecting the vital organs.

2 **The spine is made up of 26 bones, but what are they called?**

◆ Vertebrae

These strong bones help support your weight. They have special holes in them for the spinal cord to get through.

3 **Put these bones in the order they appear from top to bottom in a human skeleton:**

▲ Skull

■ Humerus

◆ Pelvis

● Femur

4 **True or false: Blood cells are produced in bone marrow.**

◆ True

Red blood cells carry oxygen, which helps the body's cells carry out their jobs.

5 **How many bones make up the adult skeleton?**

● 206

Protecting all of your organs and supporting you to move around freely requires a lot of bones.

6 Where can you find the smallest bones in the human body?

▲ Ear

Three tiny bones, called the stapes, the incus, and the malleus are found in the ear. The stapes is the smallest of these.

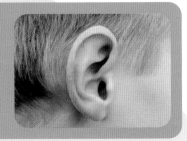

7 What's the longest bone in your body?

▲ Femur

This is the name for the thighbone. It must be strong enough to take the weight of your upper body.

8 True or false: More than half of all your bones are in your hands and feet.

◆ True

Hands and feet perform complicated tasks, so they need lots of bones for flexibility and precision.

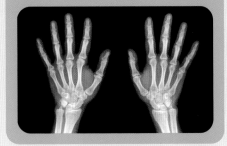

9 Which one of these is not a type of joint found in the skeleton?

◆ Slider

Four types of joints in the body are ball and socket, hinge, gliding, and pivot.

10 True or false: Human bones are completely solid structures.

▲ False

Human bones have hard outer shells but are full of spongy bone, bone marrow, and blood vessels on the inside.

Podium!

Bronze: 1–5 correct answers
Silver: 6–8 correct answers
Gold: 9–10 correct answers

Skin

Will you let this quiz get under your skin? Hopefully you won't only pass by the skin of your teeth!

1 What is the largest organ in your body?
- ◆ Liver
- ▲ Heart
- ● Skin

2 What is it called when your skin pricks up from the cold?
- ◆ Duckbumps
- ▲ Chickbumps
- ● Goosebumps

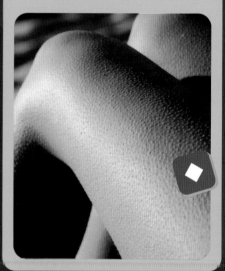

3 How many layers does your skin have?
- ◆ One
- ▲ Two
- ● Three

4 What temperature does your skin help your body keep to?
- ◆ 62.6°F (17°C)
- ▲ 80.6°F (27°C)
- ● 98.6°F (37°C)

Did you know?
The body's thinnest skin is on the eyelids, and the thickest is on the soles of the feet.

5 True or false: Skin keeps out germs and repairs itself.

◆ True

▲ False

6 What is the tough protein that helps keep your skin waterproof?

◆ Keratin

▲ Collagen

● Fibrin

7 What do your skin cells produce that helps protect you from the sun?

◆ Melanin

▲ Melanie

● Tamalin

9 Where does your sweat come from?

◆ Sweat glands

▲ Sweat veins

● Sweat pods

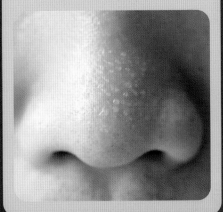

8 How many skin flakes do we lose every minute?

◆ About 10,000

▲ About 50,000

● About 100,000

10 Which one of these is not a type of touch receptor in the skin?

◆ Light pressure

▲ Heat and cold

● Stretching

■ Swelling

Turn to page 12 for the answers!

Skin

Answers

1 What is the largest organ in your body?
- Skin

In total, 16 percent of your body mass is skin.

2 What is it called when your skin pricks up from the cold?
- Goosebumps

Tiny muscles pull body hairs upright in an effort to trap warm air.

3 How many layers does your skin have?
▲ Two

The thicker dermis layer contains sweat glands and blood vessels. This is below the top layer, called the epidermis.

4 What temperature does your skin help your body keep to?
- 98.6°F (37°C)

In hot conditions your blood vessels widen to lose heat, and in cold weather they contract to retain heat.

5 True or false: Skin keeps out germs and repairs itself.
◆ True

Skin is the first defense barrier—it keeps out all sorts!

Dermis

Epidermis

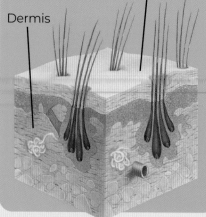

6 What is the tough protein that helps keep your skin waterproof?

◆ Keratin

Cells in the epidermis are filled with this protective protein.

7 What do your skin cells produce that helps protect you from the sun?

◆ Melanin

Special cells called melanocytes produce melanin and form a screen that blocks harmful ultraviolet rays.

8 How many skin flakes do we lose every minute?

▲ About 50,000

That results in a total of 44 lb (20 kg) of flakes in a lifetime.

9 Where does your sweat come from?

◆ Sweat glands

They produce watery sweat to cool the skin.

10 Which one of these is not a type of touch receptor in the skin?

■ Swelling

Although they do a similar job, each receptor responds most strongly to a certain type of touch.

Podium!

Bronze: 1–5 correct answers
Silver: 6–8 correct answers
Gold: 9–10 correct answers

Skull

Think you can make heads or tails of these questions? Find out how much you know about the skull.

1 **What system is the skull part of?**
◆ Respiratory
▲ Skeletal
● Cardiac

2 **What holds your head in place?**
◆ Shoulder blade
▲ Skull
● Spine

3 **True or false: In adults, only one part of the skull can move.**
◆ True
▲ False

4 **Which of the below is not a function of the skull?**
◆ To act as a cushion
▲ To protect the brain
● To support the face

5 **What part of the face is found in the "orbit" of the skull?**
◆ Ears
▲ Eyes
● Nose
■ Teeth

Did you know?

It is possible to identify someone's sex by their skull. Bone in male skulls is thicker than in female skulls.

6 How many bones are in the skull?
- ◆ 2
- ▲ 12
- ● 22
- ■ 32

7 What part of the skull contains the brain?
- ◆ Cradle
- ▲ Cranoile
- ● Cranium

8 Which part of the skull can you see in the picture below?
- ◆ Eye socket
- ▲ Jaw
- ● Nasal bones

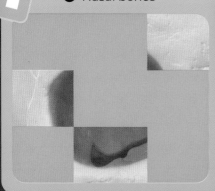

9 What is the name of the topmost vertebra?
- ◆ Axis
- ▲ Apollo
- ● Atlas
- ■ Ares

Scan the QR code for a Kahoot! about skulls.

 Turn to page 16 for the answers!

10 The place where skull bones join together is called:
- ◆ Suture
- ▲ Sewer
- ● Surface

Skull
Answers

1 What system is the skull part of?

▲ Skeletal

The skeletal system is made up of all the bones found in a human or animal body.

2 What holds your head in place?

● Spine

Your spinal column is a flexible series of bones that holds your head in an upright position.

3 True or false: In adults, only one part of the skull can move.

◆ True

The only part of the skull that can move is the lower jaw. It lets us eat, speak, and breathe.

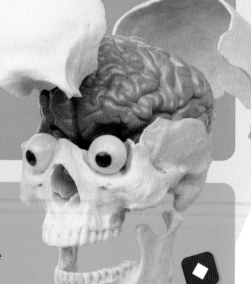

4 Which of the below is not a function of the skull?

◆ To act as a cushion

The skull is a hard protective layer that protects the brain and supports the different structures of the face.

5 What part of the face is found in the "orbit" of the skull?

▲ Eyes

The orbit is the name for the eye socket and protective bony cavity.

6 How many bones are in the skull?

● 22

The skull is made up of 22 bones. Eight make up the cranium, while the other 14 form the face.

7 What part of the skull contains the brain?

● Cranium

The main role of the cranium is to provide protection to the brain.

8 Which part of the skull can you see in the picture below?

◆ Eye socket

It is made up of seven bones.

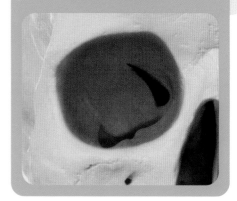

9 What is the name of the topmost vertebra?

● Atlas

The atlas is the bone at the very top of the spine. It enables the skull to nod or turn side to side.

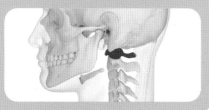

10 The place where skull bones join together is called:

● Suture

Skull bones lock together at sutures, making the skull strong.

Podium!

Bronze: 1–5 correct answers

Silver: 6–8 correct answers

Gold: 9–10 correct answers

Hair

Forget all the other parts of the body, this hair quiz is a cut above the rest!

1 **Why do humans have eyelashes?**
- ◆ To help people pull funny faces
- ▲ To look good
- ● To protect the eyes

2 **Where do hairs grow from?**
- ◆ Follicles
- ▲ Popsicles
- ● Icicles

3 **Which of these body parts do not have hair?**
- ◆ Toes
- ▲ Palms of hands
- ● Fingers

4 **How much of the body is covered in hair?**
- ◆ 25 percent
- ▲ 55 percent
- ● 75 percent
- ■ 95 percent

5 True or false: Each strand of hair is made of a cuticle, cortex, and medulla.
- ◆ True
- ▲ False

6 What is hair made from?
- ◆ Enzymes
- ▲ White blood cells
- ● Keratin
- ■ Antibodies

Did you know?

Hair grows faster during the summer. This is because blood flow to the scalp increases in warm weather.

7 What is the rarest hair color in the world?
- ◆ Blonde
- ▲ Brunette
- ● Red
- ■ Black

8 Which of these affects the color of hair?
- ◆ How much sleep someone has
- ▲ Hair temperature
- ● Levels of melanin

9 How many hairs do you shed every day?
- ◆ Less than 20
- ▲ Up to 150
- ● More than 300

10 True or false: Hairs stand on end in cold weather.
- ◆ True
- ▲ False

 Turn to page 20 for the answers!

Hair
Answers

1 **Why do humans have eyelashes?**

● To protect the eyes

Eyelash hairs have an important job to do. They stop sweat and oil dripping into the eye.

2 **Where do hairs grow from?**

◆ Follicles

These pockets in the skin house the hair root. Round follicles produce straight hair, oval follicles make wavy hair, and flat follicles produce curls.

3 **Which of these body parts do not have hair?**

▲ Palms of hands

On the outer human body, the only parts without hair are the palms of hands, soles of feet, lips, and nipples.

4 **How much of the body is covered in hair?**

■ 95 percent

Almost the whole body is covered in hair. Humans have about the same number of hair follicles as chimps.

5 **True or false: Each strand of hair is made of a cuticle, cortex, and medulla.**

◆ True

This basic hair structure is the same in each individual hair follicle.

6 What is hair made from?

● Keratin

Each hair is made from a protein called keratin. Reptile scales and bird feathers are also made of this strong substance.

7 What is the rarest hair color in the world?

● Red

The least common hair color is red, while the most common is black.

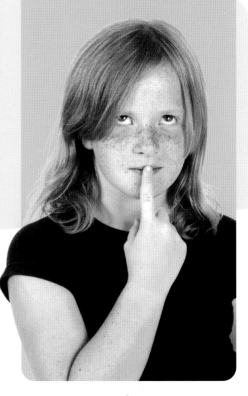

8 Which of these affects the color of hair?

● Levels of melanin

Melanin is the pigment that determines someone's hair color. More or less melanin affects the shade of the hair.

9 How many hairs do you shed every day?

▲ Up to 150

As many as 150 individual hairs are shed per day and regrown on the same day.

10 True or false: Hairs stand on end in cold weather.

◆ True

In cold weather, hairs stand on end to trap in more air and help keep mammals warm.

Podium!

Bronze: 1–5 correct answers

Silver: 6–8 correct answers

Gold: 9–10 correct answers

Brain

Time to pick your brain with these next questions all about your gray matter!

1 What allows the brain to communicate with the rest of the body?
- ◆ Elbow
- ▲ Jugular vein
- ● Spinal cord
- ■ Maxilla

2 What is the name of the cells in your brain that send important messages?
- ◆ Protons
- ▲ Neurons
- ● Electrons
- ■ Goopons

3 True or false: The brain doesn't stop forming until you are 25 years old.
- ◆ True
- ▲ False

4 What's the name of the system that controls everything you do?
- ◆ Nervous system
- ▲ Respiratory system
- ● Cardiovascular system

Did you know?

The brain changes when we learn something new. It sends messages along pathways of neurons creating new connections.

5 Put these into the order in which your brain responds:

- ◆ The body part moves.
- ▲ Brain sends signal to muscles to move.
- ● Brain calculates how to respond.
- ■ Eyes send signal based on what they see.

6 Roughly how many neurons are in the brain?

- ◆ 60 million
- ▲ 250 million
- ● 100 billion
- ■ 50 trillion

7 What's the largest part of the brain called?

- ◆ Cerebrum
- ▲ Brumbrum
- ● Certification

8 What percentage of their brain do humans use at one time?

- ◆ Less than 10 percent
- ▲ 30 percent
- ● 50 percent
- ■ Almost 100 percent

9 How much does the average brain weigh?

- ◆ 1.1 lb (0.5 kg)
- ▲ 3.3 lb (1.5 kg)
- ● 5.5 lb (2.5 kg)
- ■ 11 lb (5 kg)

Scan the QR code for a Kahoot! about brains.

Turn to page 24 for the answers!

Brain
Answers

1 **What allows the brain to communicate with the rest of the body?**

● Spinal cord

Your spinal cord runs down the center of the spine and carries nerve signals between the brain and rest of the body.

2 **What is the name of the cells in your brain that send important messages?**

▲ Neurons

These microscopic cells constantly send and receive chemical and electrical signals.

3 **True or false: The brain doesn't stop forming until you are 25 years old.**

◆ True

It triples in size in the first year of life and it doesn't reach maturity until you are 25 years old.

4 **What's the name of the system that controls everything you do?**

◆ Nervous system

It is made up of nerve cells which exist all over the body and carry messages between the various body parts.

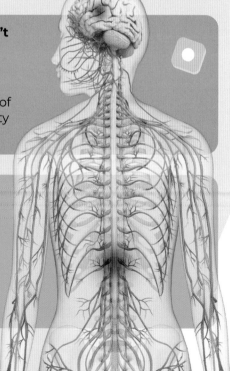

5 **Put these into the order in which your brain responds:**

- ■ Eyes send signal based on what they see.
- ● Brain calculates how to respond.
- ▲ Brain sends signal to muscles to move.
- ◆ The body part moves.

6 **Roughly how many neurons are in the brain?**

- ● 100 billion

Neuron is another word for nerve cell. These cells carry information around the body as electrical signals.

7 **What's the largest part of the brain called?**

- ◆ Cerebrum

The cerebrum has a wrinkly outer surface made of nerve cells called the cerebral cortex.

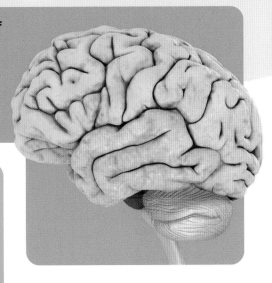

8 **What percentage of their brain do humans use at one time?**

- ■ Almost 100 percent

While many believe that only 10 percent of the brain can be used at one time, this is in fact a myth. Most of the brain is active at all times.

Podium!

Bronze: 1–4 correct answers

Silver: 5–7 correct answers

Gold: 8–9 correct answers

9 **How much does the average brain weigh?**

- ▲ 3.3 lb (1.5 kg)

The average brain weighs around the same as a half-gallon of milk.

Sight

Let's hope this quiz about eyes is a welcome sight. There's only one way to find out . . .

1 What is the colored section of the eye called?

- ◆ Ivy
- ▲ Iris
- ● Lily
- ■ Pupil

Did you know?
The pupil gets bigger when it sees something it likes the look of.

2 Why are tears important for the eye?

- ◆ To keep them sparkly
- ▲ To show emotions
- ● To keep them clean

4 How many times does the average person blink?

- ◆ 5 to 10 times per minute
- ▲ 15 to 20 times per minute
- ● 50 to 60 times per minute

3 What happens to the size of pupils in bright light?

- ◆ Get smaller
- ▲ Stay the same size
- ● Get bigger

5 What is the clear dome at the front of the eye called?
◆ Sclera
▲ Retina
● Cornea

6 True or false: Sight is the sense that gives you the most information about your surroundings.
◆ True
▲ False

7 What is the soft jelly-like substance in your eyeball called?
◆ Vitreous humor
▲ Retina
● Blood vessels
■ Macula

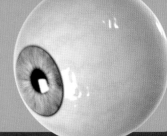

8 What connects the eye to the brain?
◆ Oblong nerve
▲ Optic nerve
● Retina nerve

9 True or false: Your eyes see things upside down.
◆ True
▲ False

10 What is the point in having eyebrows?
◆ To catch flies
▲ To frame the eyes
● To look good
■ To stop sweat landing in the eye

 Turn to page 28 for the answers!

Sight
Answers

1 **What is the colored section of the eye called?**

▲ Iris

This is where the pigments that determine eye color can be found.

2 **Why are tears important for the eye?**

● To keep them clean

Tears stop eyes drying out and protect them by flushing away dirt and irritants.

3 **What happens to the size of pupils in bright light?**

◆ Get smaller

Pupils contract in bright light to limit how much comes in. They get bigger in low light to let more light in.

4 **How many times does the average person blink?**

▲ 15 to 20 times per minute

Blinking is a reflex. In an average lifetime, that adds up to 415 million blinks.

5 **What is the clear dome at the front of the eye called?**

● Cornea

The cornea helps the eye to focus by bending light rays as they enter the eye.

6 **True or false: Sight is the sense that gives you the most information about your surroundings.**

◆ True

Your eyes gather two thirds of the information that you take in about where you are.

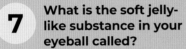

7 **What is the soft jelly-like substance in your eyeball called?**

◆ Vitreous humor

This colorless gel is mainly made of water and is found behind the lens.

8 **What connects the eye to the brain?**

▲ Optic nerve

The optic nerve contains millions of fibers and joins up the eye and the brain.

9 **True or false: Your eyes see things upside down.**

◆ True

Images the brain receives from the eyes are upside down, backwards, and two-dimensional. So it's up to your brain to flip them and make them three-dimensional.

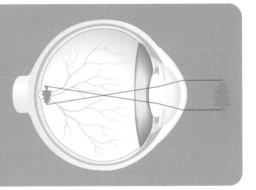

10 **What is the point in having eyebrows?**

■ To stop sweat landing in the eye

Eyebrows catch sweat before it lands in the eye, while eyelashes act as a barrier to stop dirt or dust getting into the eye.

Podium!

Bronze: 1–5 correct answers

Silver: 6–8 correct answers

Gold: 9–10 correct answers

Hearing

If you have any sense, you'll listen up. Test how much you know about hearing.

1 What does the eardrum do when it hears a noise?
- ◆ Shrinks
- ▲ Vibrates
- ● Changes color

2 How does sound enter the ear?
- ◆ Through invisible sound waves
- ▲ Through visible sound waves
- ● As a liquid

Did you know?
Some mammals, including bats and cats, can hear very high-pitched sounds that humans cannot detect.

3 Where is the eardrum?
- ◆ Bottom of the ear
- ▲ Top of the ear
- ● Outer edge of the ear
- ■ Middle of the ear

4 What is the tissue that gives the ear its shape?
- ◆ Cochlea
- ▲ Cartilage
- ● Ear canal

5 True or false: Ears help with balance.
- ◆ True
- ▲ False

6 Which part of the inner ear is this?
- ◆ Cochlea
- ▲ Eardrum
- ● Ear canal

7 What part of the ear is made up of fatty tissue?
- ◆ Pinna
- ▲ Ear canal
- ● Ear lobe

8 True or false: Ears keep themselves clean.
- ◆ True
- ▲ False

9 Why are there tiny hair cells inside the ear?
- ◆ To keep it warm
- ▲ To make it soft
- ● For picking up vibrations

10 Put these parts of the ear in the order of how sound enters the ear.
- ◆ Eardrum
- ▲ Cochlea
- ● Ossicles
- ■ Ear canal

Scan the QR code for a Kahoot! about hearing.

Turn to page 32 for the answers!

11 What are the three tiny bones within the ear called?
- ◆ Ossicles
- ▲ Riceicles
- ● Icicles

Hearing
Answers

1 **What does the eardrum do when it hears a noise?**
▲ Vibrates

The eardrum is a thin membrane that vibrates when sound reaches it.

2 **How does sound enter the ear?**
◆ Through invisible sound waves

The sound waves travel through the ear canal until they reach the eardrum.

3 **Where is the eardrum?**
■ Middle of the ear

The eardrum is a thin film that sits in the entrance to the middle ear. It helps stop things getting into your ear.

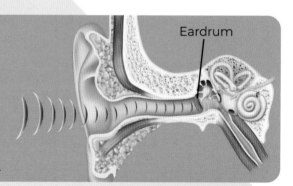

Eardrum

4 **What is the tissue that gives the ear its shape?**
▲ Cartilage

This flexible and elastic tissue gives the ear structure and shape.

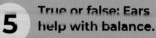

5 **True or false: Ears help with balance.**
◆ True

Sensors within the ear help with balance by sending information to the brain about the body's position.

6 **Which part of the inner ear is this?**
◆ Cochlea
In adults, it's about the size of a pea.

7 **What part of the ear is made up of fatty tissue?**
● Ear lobe
The soft, flappy part at the bottom of the ear is called the ear lobe.

8 **True or false: Ears keep themselves clean.**
◆ True
Earwax is sticky and can trap dirt or debris to stop it entering the ears.

9 **Why are there tiny hair cells inside the ear?**
● For picking up vibrations
Tiny hair cells within the ear are attached to nerves that link to the brain.

10 **Put these parts of the ear in the order of how sound enters the ear.**
■ Ear canal
◆ Eardrum
● Ossicles
▲ Cochlea

11 **What are the three tiny bones within the ear called?**
◆ Ossicles
These linked bones move back and forth when the eardrum vibrates and they're the smallest bones in the body.

Podium!
Bronze: 1–5 correct answers
Silver: 6–9 correct answers
Gold: 10–11 correct answers

Smell

Don't look down your nose at this quiz. You may just come out smelling of roses.

1 Which other sense does smell closely link to?
- ◆ Taste
- ▲ Sight
- ● Touch
- ■ Hearing

2 True or false: A human has 20 million smell receptors.
- ◆ True
- ▲ False

3 Why is it helpful for noses to pick up the scent of dangers?
- ◆ For some variety
- ▲ To warn the body to stay away
- ● To add some excitement

4 What is the smell system in the body called?
- ◆ Scented system
- ▲ Olfactory system
- ● Aroma system
- ■ Sniffy system

5 Which part of the body analyses the smells detected?

◆ Eyes

▲ Nose

● Brain

6 True or false: Men have a stronger sense of smell than women.

◆ True

▲ False

7 Is mucus ever helpful?

◆ No, it is just annoying.

▲ Yes, it makes things smell lovely.

● Yes, it traps germs and stops them entering the nose.

Did you know?
When someone is hungry, their sense of smell grows stronger.

8 Put these in order of how smells are identified in the body:

◆ Brain

▲ Smell receptors

● Odor molecules float in the air

■ Olfactory bulb

9 What happens when something unwelcome gets trapped in the nose?

◆ Coughing

▲ Sneezing

● Blinking

■ Snoring

10 How many different scents can humans smell?

◆ One thousand

▲ One million

● One billion

■ One trillion

 Turn to page 36 for the answers!

Smell
Answers

1 **Which other sense does smell closely link to?**

◆ Taste

Smell and taste work together so that we can experience a full sense of flavor and scent.

2 **True or false: A human has 20 million smell receptors.**

◆ True

Molecules in the air attach to smell receptors in the nose and send a message to the brain.

3 **Why is it helpful for noses to pick up the scent of dangers?**

▲ To warn the body to stay away

Smells like smoke can warn us of danger. The smell of food that has gone off lets us know not to eat it.

4 **What is the smell system in the body called?**

▲ Olfactory system

The olfactory system is made up of structures that work together to form someone's sense of smell.

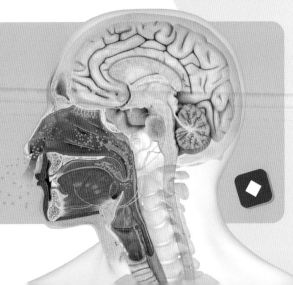

5 **Which part of the body analyses the smells detected?**

● Brain

Nerves send the information from the receptor cells to the brain.

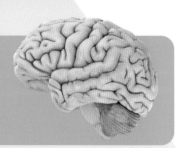

6 **True or false: Men have a stronger sense of smell than women.**

▲ False

Research shows that women have more cells in their olfactory bulb and this makes their sense of smell stronger than men's.

7 **Is mucus ever helpful?**

● Yes, it traps germs and stops them entering the nose.

Mucus is produced in the mucous membrane and acts as a barrier to stop irritants entering the lungs.

9 **What happens when something unwelcome gets trapped in the nose?**

▲ Sneezing

Dust or particles can be dislodged from the nose by sneezing.

8 **Put these in order of how smells are identified in the body:**

● Odor molecules float in the air

▲ Smell receptors

■ Olfactory bulb

◆ Brain

10 **How many different scents can humans smell?**

■ One trillion

Each odor breathed in activates receptors in the nose differently, allowing us to distinguish scent.

Podium!

Bronze: 1–5 correct answers

Silver: 6–8 correct answers

Gold: 9–10 correct answers

Taste

Hungry for another quiz?
Then chomp through this
bite-sized quiz about taste!

1 **What action helps release taste chemicals into the taste buds?**
- ◆ Sleeping
- ▲ Dancing
- ● Chewing
- ■ Breathing

2 **Why are humans attracted to sweet food?**
- ◆ It looks pretty.
- ▲ The colors are tempting.
- ● It's easier to digest.
- ■ It gives us energy.

3 **How many different tastes are there?**
- ◆ Two
- ▲ Three
- ● Four
- ■ Five

4 **As well as helping us enjoy delicious food, taste also . . .**
- ◆ Warns us when something is burning
- ▲ Warns us when food is rotten
- ● Tells us when we're hungry
- ■ Helps us sleep

5 How many taste buds are found on a child's tongue?

- ◆ 50
- ▲ 100
- ● 1,000
- ■ 10,000

6 How many salivary glands are in the mouth?

- ◆ Two
- ▲ Four
- ● Six
- ■ Eight

Did you know?

Humans have fewer taste buds than dogs and cats. Because of this, water tastes less flavorful to people than it does to our furry friends.

7 True or false: Only the front of the tongue can detect bitter tastes.

- ◆ True
- ▲ False

8 How does information get sent from taste cells to the brain?

- ◆ Nerve fibers
- ▲ In the blood
- ● It's inhaled

9 Sense of taste is part of the . . .

- ◆ Gustatory system
- ▲ Respiratory system
- ● Cardiac system

Scan the QR code for a Kahoot! about taste.

Turn to page 40 for the answers!

10 Why is the tongue covered in bumps called "papillae"?

- ◆ They make patterns in the food.
- ▲ They mash up the food.
- ● They help to grip food.

Taste

Answers

1 **What action helps release taste chemicals into the taste buds?**

● Chewing

The action of chewing breaks down food and releases chemicals that then dissolve in the mouth's saliva and seep into taste buds.

2 **Why are humans attracted to sweet food?**

■ It gives us energy.

High-sugar food is appealing to us because it gives us a boost of energy.

3 **How many different tastes are there?**

■ Five

The five tastes are sour, bitter, salty, sweet, and umami.

4 **As well as helping us enjoy delicious food, taste also . . .**

▲ Warns us when food is rotten

Taste helps us to detect when food is past its best and may cause us harm or make us sick.

5 **How many taste buds are found on a child's tongue?**

■ 10,000

A whopping 10,000 taste buds are found on the tongue to receive the various flavors.

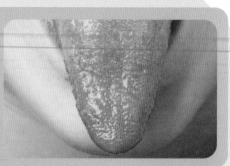

6 How many salivary glands are in the mouth?

● Six

The salivary glands on each side of the mouth constantly produce saliva to help digestion.

7 True or false: Only the front of the tongue can detect bitter tastes.

▲ False

Tastes, including bitter, can be sensed all over the tongue.

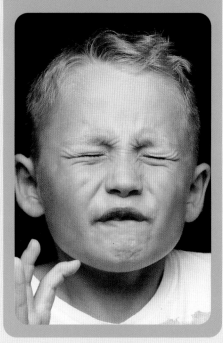

8 How does information get sent from taste cells to the brain?

◆ Nerve fibers

The signals sent to the brain via nerve fibers help the brain to figure out the taste.

9 Sense of taste is part of the . . .

◆ Gustatory system

The word "gustatory" means something to do with taste or tasting.

10 Why is the tongue covered in bumps called "papillae"?

● They help to grip food.

Bumpy papillae make the surface of the tongue rough, which provides grip.

Podium!

Bronze: 1–5 correct answers
Silver: 6–8 correct answers
Gold: 9–10 correct answers

Eating

Get chomping and munching, that's the way to consume this page of quiz questions!

1 Food provides the body with . . .
◆ Nutrients
▲ Molecules

2 Which of these foods is not a carbohydrate?
◆ Pasta
▲ Bread
● Meat

3 Which of these nutrients helps the body build new cells?
◆ Carbohydrates
▲ Proteins
● Fats
■ Vitamins

4 True or false: During an average lifetime, a person will consume at least 22 tons (20 tonnes) of food.
◆ True
▲ False

5 All your energy comes from food and drink. The energy you get from food or drink is measured in what?
◆ Kilowatts
▲ Calories

6
Which of these is not a vitamin?

◆ Vitamin A
▲ Vitamin C
● Vitamin D
■ Vitamin X

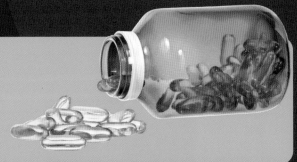

Did you know?

Some foods contain a lot of water. For example, apples are 84 percent water.

7
How does the mineral calcium help your body?

◆ Strengthens your teeth and bones
▲ Gives you stronger muscles
● Keeps your heart pumping

9
How many glasses of water should you drink a day?

◆ 4–6
▲ 6–8
● 20–25

8
Put these foods in order of how many calories they contain.

◆ An apple
▲ A bagel
● A pepper

10
What does your stomach do that makes you feel hungry?

◆ It releases a hormone.
▲ It expands.
● It makes you feel sick.

Turn to page 44 for the answers!

Eating

Answers

1 Food provides the body with . . .
◆ Nutrients
These can only be released from food once it has gone through the process of digestion.

2 Which of these foods is not a carbohydrate?
● Meat
Pasta and bread are starchy foods containing carbohydrates, which give you energy.

3 Which of these nutrients helps the body build new cells?
▲ Proteins
Nuts, meat, fish, eggs, tofu, beans, and pulses are all good sources of protein.

4 True or false: During an average lifetime, a person will consume at least 22 tons (20 tonnes) of food.
◆ True!
Adult men have an average daily intake of 2,550 calories.

5 All your energy comes from food and drink. The energy you get from food or drink is measured in what?
▲ Calories
If you regularly eat more calories than your body uses, the extra energy is stored as fat.

6 Which of these is not a vitamin?

■ Vitamin X

Vitamins are essential for good health. A healthy diet should include vitamins A, B group, C, D, and E.

7 How does the mineral calcium help your body?

◆ Strengthens your teeth and bones

You need enough vitamin D in your body to make sure calcium is absorbed from your small intestine.

9 How many glasses of water should you drink a day?

▲ 6–8

A good daily intake of water is essential for your body.

8 Put these foods in order of how many calories they contain.

● A pepper: 30 calories

◆ An apple: 100 calories

▲ A bagel: 250 calories

Calories are used as the measurement of energy that a particular food or drink provides.

10 What does your stomach do that makes you feel hungry?

◆ It releases a hormone.

Hunger and fullness are sensations produced by a part of your brain called the hypothalamus.

Podium!

Bronze: 1–5 correct answers

Silver: 6–8 correct answers

Gold: 9–10 correct answers

Digestion

Do you have the stomach for this digestion quiz? Find out whether going with your gut will pay off.

1 When does the digestive process begin?
- ◆ Before you eat
- ▲ When you eat
- ● After you've eaten

2 What organ is sometimes called the "gullet"?
- ◆ Stomach
- ▲ Esophagus
- ● Mouth

3 True or false: The stomach breaks down food.
- ◆ True
- ▲ False

4 Put these organs in the order that food moves through them when you eat:
- ◆ Small intestine
- ▲ Esophagus
- ● Large intestine
- ■ Mouth

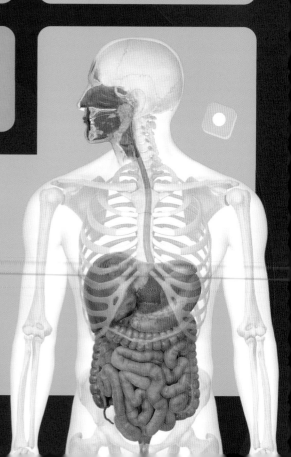

Did you know?

It takes 24 hours for a sandwich to move through your digestive system.

---

5 How long is your gut from start to finish?
- ◆ 7 ft (2 m)
- ▲ 16 ft (5 m)
- ● 30 ft (9 m)

---

6 What is the name of the protein in our bodies that speeds up metabolism?
- ◆ Antibodies
- ▲ Enzymes
- ● Meat

7 What is the name of the wave-like motion that pushes food along the esophagus?
- ◆ Wavestalsis
- ▲ Ripplestalsis
- ● Peristalsis

---

8 One of the jobs of the liver is to . . .
- ◆ Get rid of toxins
- ▲ Add saliva
- ● Make food tastier

Scan the QR code for a Kahoot! about digestion.

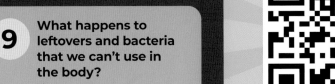

---

9 What happens to leftovers and bacteria that we can't use in the body?
- ◆ They go through the digestive process again.
- ▲ They turn into hair.
- ● They are excreted as waste.

Turn to page 48 for the answers!

Digestion
Answers

1 When does the digestive process begin?

◆ Before you eat

The smell, sight, or thought of food kickstarts the digestive process and saliva forms in your mouth.

2 What organ is sometimes called the "gullet"?

▲ Esophagus

This hollow, muscular tube sits behind the windpipe and connects the throat to the stomach.

3 True or false: The stomach breaks down food.

◆ True

Food mixes with digestive juices in the stomach that begin to break down food.

4 Put these organs in the order that food moves through them when you eat:

■ Mouth
▲ Esophagus
◆ Small intestine
● Large intestine

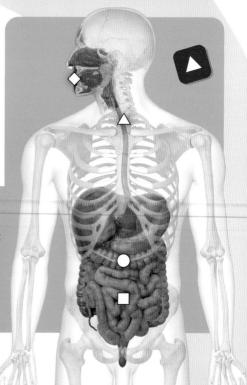

5 How long is your gut from start to finish?

● 30 ft (9 m)

That's about the same length as a bus!

6 What is the name of the protein in our bodies that speeds up metabolism?

▲ Enzymes

Digestive enzymes are produced in the stomach, small intestine, and pancreas to break down carbohydrates, proteins, and fats.

7 What is the name of the wave-like motion that pushes food along the esophagus?

● Peristalsis

Muscles in the esophagus use wave-like movement to push the food into the stomach.

8 One of the jobs of the liver is to . . .

◆ Get rid of toxins

The liver redirects nutrients and gets rid of any harmful substances that are in the body.

9 What happens to leftovers and bacteria that we can't use in the body?

● They are excreted as waste.

After food and drink are digested and pass through the large intestines, the body expels waste products.

Podium!

Bronze: 1–4 correct answers

Silver: 5–7 correct answers

Gold: 8–9 correct answers

Staying Healthy

How much do you know about staying fit and healthy? Test your knowledge with this quiz.

1 Which one of these is not needed for a healthy body?
- ◆ Sleep
- ▲ Vitamins
- ● Minerals
- ■ Cookies

2 To stay healthy, what should a person eat?
- ◆ Food that's all the same color
- ▲ A wide variety of food
- ● Mostly vegetables
- ■ Mostly dairy

3 What mineral is vital for healthy teeth?
- ◆ Iron
- ▲ Calcium
- ● Bicarbonate
- ■ Phosphorus

4 What food is high in vitamin C and can help boost the immune system?
- ◆ Meat
- ▲ Citrus fruit
- ● Dairy

5 When are muscles able to relax and restore?
- ◆ During sleep
- ▲ During exercise
- ● At dinner time
- ■ On a long walk

6 When a super-fit person exercises, their heart needs to work . . .

◆ Even harder than someone who is unfit

▲ Less hard than someone who is unfit

● The same as someone who is unfit

7 What vitamin is produced by being in sunlight?

◆ Vitamin C

▲ Vitamin D

● Vitamin A

Did you know?
During deep sleep, people cannot cough or sneeze because most muscles are paralyzed during dreams.

8 Which of the below is not a way that the body tries to rid itself of germs?

◆ Sneezing

▲ Coughing

● Snoring

9 True or false: The fitter you are, the slower your resting heartbeat.

◆ True

▲ False

10 What activity would not help someone stay healthy?

◆ Gardening

▲ Going to the gym

● Eating fast food

Turn to page 52 for the answers!

Staying Healthy
Answers

1 **Which one of these is not needed for a healthy body?**

■ Cookies

The right amount of sleep, vitamins, and minerals are all important for maintaining a healthy body and lifestyle.

2 **To stay healthy, what should a person eat?**

▲ A wide variety of food

Eating a varied diet involves eating food from as many food groups as you can.

3 **What mineral is vital for healthy teeth?**

▲ Calcium

Stored in the bones, calcium helps keep teeth strong and healthy.

4 **What food is high in vitamin C and can help boost the immune system?**

▲ Citrus fruit

Eating fruit such as lemons, oranges, and grapefruit are a good way to keep up vitamin C levels.

5 **When are muscles able to relax and restore?**

◆ During sleep

Muscles are constantly working, so it's vital they can rest up and have a chance to repair during the night.

6 When a super-fit person exercises, their heart needs to work . . .

▲ Less hard than someone who is unfit

When a person is fit and healthy, the heart can do its job with less effort.

7 What vitamin is produced by being in sunlight?

▲ Vitamin D

In sunlight, the skin produces vitamin D which is needed for strong and healthy bones.

8 Which of the below is not a way that the body tries to rid itself of germs?

● Snoring

Coughing and sneezing are the body's way of clearing out dust and germs, whereas snoring has no purpose.

9 True or false: The fitter you are, the slower your resting heartbeat.

◆ True

A healthy heart needs to beat less hard to supply the body with oxygen and fuel. A normal resting heart rate is between 40 and 100 beats per minute.

Podium!

Bronze: 1–5 correct answers

Silver: 6–8 correct answers

Gold: 9–10 correct answers

10 What activity would not help someone stay healthy?

● Eating fast food

Fast food is often high in saturated fats, sugar, and salt. Both gardening and the gym would support an active lifestyle and help keep someone fit.

Teeth

It's time to sink your gnashers into this next quiz all about teeth!

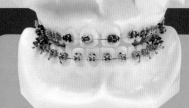

1 How many sets of teeth does a human have in their lifetime?
- ◆ One
- ▲ Two
- ● Three

2 Why do some people wear braces?
- ◆ To help them eat
- ▲ To clean their mouth
- ● To straighten teeth

3 What is the name of the white substance that covers teeth?
- ◆ Enamel
- ▲ Chalk
- ● Edamame

4 What is the job of the wide and sturdy teeth at the back?
- ◆ Tearing food
- ▲ Crushing and grinding up food
- ● Adding flavor

5 How many teeth does an adult have?
- ◆ 20
- ▲ 22
- ● 30
- ■ 32

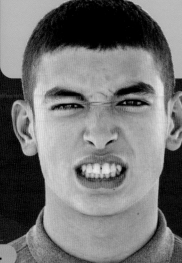

6 Why might a dentist give someone a filling in their tooth?
- ◆ To make them look nice
- ▲ Teeth are too far apart
- ● Tooth decay

Did you know?
People spend a total of 38 days on average brushing their teeth during their lifetime.

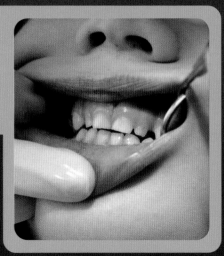

7 Which mineral is beneficial to teeth?
- ◆ Sodium
- ▲ Copper
- ● Calcium

8 What is plaque?
- ◆ A buildup of food and bacteria
- ▲ An ingredient found in toothpaste
- ● An enzyme found in the mouth

9 Which food could damage tooth enamel?
- ◆ Meat
- ▲ Milk
- ● Fruit

Scan the QR code for a Kahoot! about teeth.

10 Which teeth don't grow through until someone is at least 17 years old?
- ◆ Wisdom teeth
- ▲ Wise teeth
- ● Milk teeth

Turn to page 56 for the answers!

Teeth
Answers

1 How many sets of teeth does a human have in their lifetime?

▲ Two

The first set are known as "milk teeth," which young children have. These are later replaced by adult teeth.

2 Why do some people wear braces?

● To straighten teeth

An orthodontist might fit a brace to treat irregularities in teeth and jaws.

3 What is the name of the white substance that covers teeth?

◆ Enamel

Teeth are coated in enamel, which protects them from erosion.

4 What is the job of the wide and sturdy teeth at the back?

▲ Crushing and grinding up food

The wide teeth at the back are called molars. They have the power needed to grind up food.

5 How many teeth does an adult have?

■ 32

A child has 20 milk teeth and these are replaced with 32 adult teeth.

6 Why might a dentist give someone a filling in their tooth?

● Tooth decay

When plaque builds up on teeth, it releases acid and this damages tooth enamel.

7 Which mineral is beneficial to teeth?

● Calcium

Food rich in calcium, such as dairy, helps teeth defend against erosion.

8 What is plaque?

◆ A buildup of food and bacteria

Plaque builds up on a tooth's surface when it's not cleaned properly. Regularly brushing and flossing prevents this from happening.

9 Which food could damage tooth enamel?

● Fruit

It's fine to eat fruit as part of a balanced diet, as long as you brush your teeth carefully.

10 Which teeth don't grow through until someone is at least 17 years old?

◆ Wisdom teeth

Found right at the back of the mouth, wisdom teeth appear when someone is 17 or older, or sometimes they don't ever appear.

Podium!

Bronze: 1–5 correct answers

Silver: 6–8 correct answers

Gold: 9–10 correct answers

Scans

Do you know an ultrasound from an X-ray? Scan this page of questions and get ready to answer this quiz!

1 What discovery made it possible to develop techniques to see into the human body?
- ◆ DNA testing
- ▲ Stem cell transplants
- ● X-ray

2 If you wanted to see down into your stomach, how would you do it?
- ◆ Have an X-ray
- ▲ Have an endoscopy
- ● Have an MEG scan

3 Soft tissue like body organs can't be X-rayed, so how do we get pictures of them?
- ◆ Ultrawave
- ▲ Ultra-ray
- ● Ultrasound

4 True or false: A technique called SPECT can show how your blood is flowing. It works with a type of radiation using gamma rays.
- ◆ True
- ▲ False

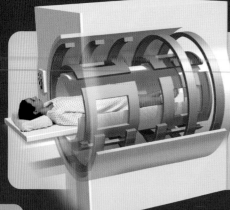

5 What does MRI (a type of scan) stand for?
- ◆ Magnetic resonance imaging
- ▲ Major resource incident
- ● Main radioactive inlet

6 How can you see a fetus inside a mother's womb?

◆ Using an endoscope

▲ You can't!

● Ultrasound

■ MRI

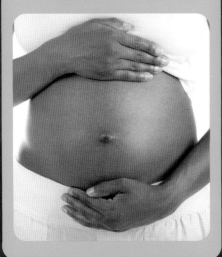

7 Can you see what your brain is thinking by scanning it?

◆ Yes

▲ No

9 In the world of human body scans, what is a PET?

◆ A new puppy!

▲ Position emission tomography

● Private energy tower

Did you know?

Your body's tissue gives off radio waves when stimulated by powerful MRI magnets, which help to create detailed pictures of your body in MRI scans.

8 Can you use 2D scans to form 3D scans?

◆ Yes

▲ No

Turn to page 60 for the answers!

Scans

Answers

1 What discovery made it possible to develop techniques to see into the human body?

● X-ray

Since the discovery of X-rays, many more methods of looking inside the body have been developed.

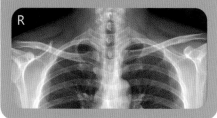

2 If you wanted to see down into your stomach, how would you do it?

▲ Have an endoscopy

An endoscope is a thin, flexible tube with a camera at the end.

3 Soft tissue like body organs can't be X-rayed, so how do we get pictures of them?

● Ultrasound

This scanning technique makes images from sound waves.

4 True or false: A technique called SPECT can show how your blood is flowing. It works with a type of radiation using gamma rays.

◆ True

SPECT stands for single-photon emission computed tomography!

5 What does MRI (a type of scan) stand for?

◆ Magnetic resonance imaging

Scanners use powerful magnets to stimulate the body's tissues, which causes them to give off radio waves.

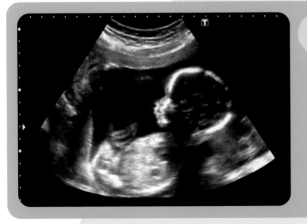

6 How can you see a fetus inside a mother's womb?

● Ultrasound

Many ultrasound scanners are small enough to use by hand to check on babies in the uterus.

7 Can you see what your brain is thinking by scanning it?

◆ Yes

MEG scanners record electric currents in the brain, and the magnetic forces they generate. The readings produce digital images of the brain in action.

8 Can you use 2D scans to form 3D scans?

◆ Yes

CT scanners rotate around a person and make X-ray images of 2D "slices" of the body. These images can be layered on top of each other to produce more helpful 3D images.

9 In the world of human body scans, what is a PET?

▲ Position emission tomography

Radioactive chemicals are injected into the body. These show high and low levels of cell activity, and can detect cancers.

Podium!

Bronze: 1–4 correct answers
Silver: 5–7 correct answers
Gold: 8–9 correct answers

Breathing

Did you nose-dive in the last quiz? Take a deep breath and try this next quiz.

1 What is the process of breathing called?
- ◆ Respiration
- ▲ Reproduction
- ● Metabolism

2 What is the other name for your windpipe?
- ◆ Flute
- ▲ Trachea
- ● Trapeze

3 Does the ribcage expand when you breathe in?
- ◆ Yes
- ▲ No

4 True or false: Humans take in nitrogen and get rid of oxygen when they breathe.
- ◆ True
- ▲ False

5 What can you see in this picture?
- ◆ Ravioli
- ▲ Alveoli
- ● Alvini

6 What is the dome-shaped sheet of muscle below your lungs?

◆ Biceps

▲ Calves

● Diaphragm

Did you know?
When you exhale, you breathe out water as well as air—about 0.6 fl oz (17.5 ml) of water per hour, but more if you're exercising.

7 How many breaths do you take every day on average?

◆ 500

▲ 10,000

● 40,000

8 True or false: Plants breathe in the same way as humans.

◆ True

▲ False

9 What does the air we breathe out contain?

◆ More oxygen and less carbon dioxide

▲ Less oxygen and more carbon dioxide

10 What is the name of the tiny tubes in your lungs that warm air as you breathe?

◆ Bronchioles

▲ Broccoli

● Brine

Scan the QR code for a Kahoot! about breathing.

11 What is not good for your lungs?

◆ Dancing

▲ Reading

● Smoking

■ Snorkeling

Turn to page 64 for the answers!

Breathing Answers

1 **What is the process of breathing called?**

◆ Respiration

This is the process that takes in oxygen and discharges carbon dioxide.

2 **What is the other name for your windpipe?**

▲ Trachea

Air travels in and out of the body via a tube known as the trachea.

3 **Does the ribcage expand when you breathe in?**

◆ Yes

When you breathe in, the muscles between your ribs tighten and pull the bones up and out.

4 **True or false: Humans take in nitrogen and get rid of oxygen.**

▲ False

Humans take in oxygen by breathing in, and then they release the waste carbon dioxide by breathing out.

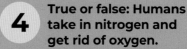

5 **What can you see in this picture?**

▲ Alveoli

This is the name for the bunches of microscopic airbags found at the end of the bronchioles.

6 What is the dome-shaped sheet of muscle below your lungs?

● Diaphragm

This sheet of muscle pulls down the lungs as you breathe in.

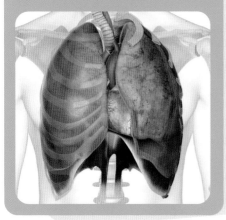

7 How many breaths do you take every day on average?

● 40,000

We breathe in and out between 12 and 15 times a minute.

8 True or false: Plants breathe in the same way as humans.

▲ False

Plants absorb air through their leaves, but humans breathe air through their mouths and into their lungs.

9 What does the air we breathe out contain?

▲ Less oxygen and more carbon dioxide

The oxygen we breathe in passes into the blood and is carried around the body.

10 What is the name of the tiny tubes in your lungs that warm air as you breathe?

◆ Bronchioles

Their job is to warm, moisten, and clean the inhaled air.

11 What is not good for your lungs?

● Smoking

The airways and small air sacs within the lungs can be damaged by the toxins inhaled from smoking.

Podium!

Bronze: 1–5 correct answers

Silver: 6–9 correct answers

Gold: 10–11 correct answers

Muscles

Find out if your brain muscles are big enough to ace this quiz.

1 **How many types of muscles do you have?**
- ◆ 1
- ▲ 2
- ● 3

2 **Your core muscles stop you . . .**
- ◆ Flopping forward at the waist when you bend over
- ▲ Shrinking and getting smaller
- ● Eating too much when you're full

3 **How much of your body weight is made up by the big muscles that cover your skeleton?**
- ◆ Quarter
- ▲ Half
- ● Three quarters

4 **The back has three main muscle layers. What from the list below do they not do?**
- ◆ Help with breathing
- ▲ Stabilize and move the torso
- ● Help you to swallow

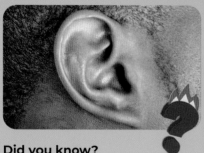

Did you know?
About 20 percent of humans can wiggle their ears voluntarily, using the auricularis muscles.

5 What's the most powerful muscle in your body?
◆ Bicep
▲ Masseter
● Calf

6 What's the fastest muscles in your body?
◆ Leg muscles
▲ Eyeball muscles
● Arm muscles
■ Neck muscles

7 How many more muscles than bones do you have in your body?
◆ Two times
▲ Three times
● Ten times
■ Fifty times

8 True or false: A muscle can pull, but it can't push.
◆ True
▲ False

9 How many muscles do you have in your tongue?
◆ 2
▲ 8
● 14

10 How many muscles does it take to move your fingers and thumb?
◆ About 3
▲ About 13
● About 30

 Turn to page 68 for the answers!

Muscles
Answers

1 **How many types of muscles do you have?**

● 3

You use skeletal muscles to move your arms and legs, heart muscle to power your heart, and smooth muscle to move food along your digestive system.

2 **Your core muscles stop you . . .**

◆ Flopping forward at the waist when you bend over

Core muscles are a group of muscles that also protect your spine and help with healthy balance and posture.

3 **How much of your body weight is made up by the big muscles that cover your skeleton?**

▲ Half

They form layers that work together to move all parts of your body.

4 **The back has three main muscle layers. What from the list below do they not do?**

● Help you to swallow

This is done by tongue and the throat muscles.

5 **What's the most powerful muscle in your body?**

▲ Masseter

The masseter muscle is in your jaw and you use it to chew food.

6 **What's the fastest muscles in your body?**

▲ Eyeball muscles

They shift your gaze in about two-hundredths of a second.

7 **How many more muscles than bones do you have in your body?**

▲ Three times

You have about 600 muscles in your body.

8 **True or false: A muscle can pull, but it can't push.**

◆ True

When a muscle is stimulated by a nerve signal, it contracts and gets shorter. It cannot make itself longer.

9 **How many muscles do you have in your tongue?**

● 14

Its flexibility helps you eat and speak.

10 **How many muscles does it take to move your fingers and thumb?**

● About 30

Many are located in your forearm and are attached to your hand bones by tough, cord-like straps that are called tendons.

Podium!

Bronze: 1–5 correct answers

Silver: 6–8 correct answers

Gold: 9–10 correct answers

Heart

It's no use being half-hearted when it comes to taking on these questions.

1 How does blood travel around the body?

◆ By boat
▲ In blood vessels
● In hairs

2 How many chambers does the heart have?

◆ Two
▲ Four
● Six

3 True or false: The sound of a heartbeat is the valves closing.

◆ True
▲ False

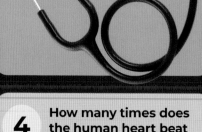

4 How many times does the human heart beat in an average lifetime?

◆ 2,500 million
▲ 35,000 million
● 90,000 million

Did you know?

The double-walled layer of tissue surrounding the heart is called the pericardium. It keeps infections out and stops the heart from rubbing against other organs.

5 A human heart is the size of a . . .
- ◆ Foot
- ▲ Fist
- ● Tomato

6 How much blood does each heartbeat pump out?
- ◆ 1 fl oz (30 ml)
- ▲ 2.3 fl oz (70 ml)
- ● 1 pt (500 ml)
- ■ 1.8 pts (1 liter)

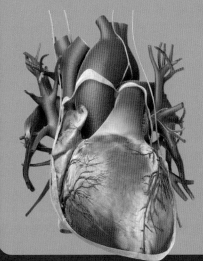

7 What carries oxygenated blood to the other organs?
- ◆ Veins
- ▲ Arteries
- ● Capillaries

8 Which group of people has the fastest heartbeat?
- ◆ Elderly
- ▲ Young adults
- ● Newborn babies

9 How many pints of blood does the average adult have in their body?
- ◆ 5 pints (3 liters)
- ▲ 10 pints (6 liters)
- ● 20 pints (11 liters)

10 Which artery carries blood to the rest of the body?
- ◆ Aorta
- ▲ Vena cava
- ● Coronary

Scan the QR code for a Kahoot! about hearts.

Turn to page 72 for the answers!

Heart

Answers

1 How does blood travel around the body?

▲ In blood vessels

Arteries, veins, and capillaries are all types of blood vessel.

2 How many chambers does the heart have?

▲ Four

The heart is divided into four sections: left atrium, left ventricle, right atrium, right ventricle.

3 True or false: The sound of a heartbeat is the valves closing.

◆ True

The rhythmic sound made by the heart is the result of the valves slamming shut.

4 How many times does the human heart beat in an average lifetime?

◆ 2,500 million

When resting, your heart beats between 40 and 100 times per minute. This measure is abbreviated to bpm (beats per minute).

5 A human heart is the size of a . . .

▲ Fist

The fist-sized organ is found to the left side of the body.

6
How much blood does each heartbeat pump out?

▲ 2.3 fl oz (70 ml)

The heart beats once a second and pushes 2.3 fl oz (70 ml) of blood around the body and refills for the next beat.

7
What carries oxygenated blood to the other organs?

▲ Arteries

The arteries carry oxygenated blood away from the heart and to the other organs in the body.

8
Which group of people has the fastest heartbeat?

■ Newborn babies

Up to one month old, babies' heart rates are 70 to 190 beats per minute (bpm). By 10 years old, it slows to 60 to 100 bpm.

9
How many pints of blood does the average adult have in their body?

▲ 10 pints (6 liters)

Adults have around 10 pints (6 liters) of blood in their body, which makes up 8 percent of their total body weight.

10
Which artery carries blood to the rest of the body?

◆ Aorta

The body's main artery carries oxygenated blood from the heart to the rest of the body.

Podium!

Bronze: 1–5 correct answers

Silver: 6–8 correct answers

Gold: 9–10 correct answers

Movement

Don't stop moving—unless you need to sit still and do this quiz!

1 What makes you move?
- ◆ Nerve signals from your brain.
- ▲ Your eyes tell your brain.
- ● It just comes naturally.

2 Which of these movements are unconscious?
- ◆ Heartbeat
- ▲ Running
- ● Blinking your eyes
- ■ Nodding your head

3 How do your ears help you keep moving?
- ◆ Help keep your balance
- ▲ Help you go faster
- ● Help you walk taller

4 Which bone supports your head and body, and allows you to twist and bend?
- ◆ Your spine
- ▲ Your collarbone
- ● Your ribs

5 Put the movements for throwing a ball in the correct order:
- ◆ Snapping forward
- ▲ Following through
- ● Preparing to throw

Did you know?
The brain takes 0.03 seconds to send messages to the muscles to correct the body if you start to lose your balance.

6 True or false: The nerve cells that carry the electrical impulses from your brain to your muscles are called motor neurons.

◆ True

▲ False

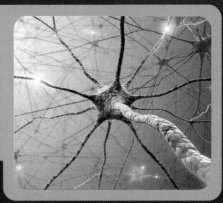

7 How many different expressions can you make with your face?

◆ 70

▲ 700

● 7,000

8 What system is not involved in every single movement your body makes?

◆ Cardiovascular system

▲ Digestive system

● Muscular system

9 What's the place called where signals from the brain are passed via nerves to muscle fibers to tell them to move?

◆ Nerve-muscle junction

▲ Nerve-muscle crossways

● Nerve-muscle intersection

10 How far will the average person walk in their lifetime?

◆ 36,000 miles (58,000 km)

▲ 48,500 miles (78,000 km)

● 80,000 miles (128,000 km)

Turn to page 76 for the answers!

Movement
Answers

1 **What makes you move?**
- ◆ Nerve signals from your brain

Your brain sends messages through your spinal cord to your muscles.

2 **Which of these movements are unconscious?**
- ◆ Heartbeat
- ● Blinking your eyes

The other two are movements that you consciously choose to do.

3 **How do your ears help you keep moving?**
- ◆ Help keep your balance

The balance sensors in your ears send signals to your brain.

4 **Which bone supports your head and body, and allows you to twist and bend?**
- ◆ Your spine

This column of bones holds your head and body up and protects your delicate spinal cord.

5 Put the movements for throwing a ball in the correct order:
- ● Preparing to throw
- ◆ Snapping forward
- ▲ Following through

The muscles in the back, shoulder, and arm pull the arm back. The shoulder joint rotates and then the arm goes down and the shoulder rotates further.

6 True or false: The nerve cells that carry the electrical impulses from your brain to your muscles are called motor neurons.

◆ True

Nerve signals can travel along nerves at up to 217 mph (350 kph).

8 What system is not involved in every single movement your body makes?

▲ Digestive system

The muscular system needs the cardiovascular system, as without blood flow to muscles, the muscles cannot move.

7 How many different expressions can you make with your face?

● 7,000

Some of them only last a fraction of a second.

9 What's the place called where signals from the brain are passed via nerves to muscle fibers to tell them to move?

◆ Nerve-muscle junction

These signals are carried from your brain by neurons inside nerves linked to your muscles.

10 How far will the average person walk in their lifetime?

● 80,000 miles (128,000 km)

That's the same as walking round the world three times!

Podium!

Bronze: 1–5 correct answers
Silver: 6–8 correct answers
Gold: 9–10 correct answers

Exercise

Get ready to limber up and put your knowledge to the test with this exercise quiz.

1 Where does the body get energy from to exercise?
- ◆ Sunlight
- ▲ Food
- ● Music

2 What are the two main types of exercise?
- ◆ Easy and hard
- ▲ Aerobic and anaerobic
- ● Indoor and outdoor

3 Resistance training is a form of exercise that . . .
- ◆ Involves fishing
- ▲ Makes hair grow
- ● Builds muscle
- ■ Builds houses

4 True or false: Women need more calories than men.
- ◆ True
- ▲ False

5 What happens to the heart during exercise?
- ◆ Stays the same as usual
- ▲ Beats slower
- ● Beats faster

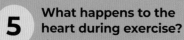

6 Which of these is not a type of aerobic exercise?
- ◆ Cycling
- ▲ Swimming
- ● Weight lifting

7 True or false: Brain cells work more effectively after exercise.

◆ True

▲ False

Did you know?

Regular exercise can boost mood, give people more energy, and help to treat depression or anxiety.

8 Why is it important to drink plenty of water when working out?

◆ It's a nice excuse for a break.

▲ A water bottle is a cool accessory.

● Lots of fluids are lost when sweating.

9 During exercise, breathing increases from 15 times per minute to up to . . .

◆ 20 times per minute

▲ 30 times per minute

● 60 times per minute

Scan the QR code for a Kahoot! about exercise.

10 Which activity will use up the most energy?

◆ Sleeping

▲ Sitting at a desk

● Watching television

■ Star jumping

Turn to page 80 for the answers!

Exercise
Answers

1 Where does the body get energy from to exercise?
▲ Food
Food provides fuel to the body so it can move around. Exercising uses up food energy.

2 What are the two main types of exercise?
▲ Aerobic and anaerobic
Aerobic is longer periods of movement, like running. Anaerobic is shorter bursts of movement, like sprinting or jumping.

3 Resistance training is a form of exercise that . . .
● Builds muscle
Exercises that repeatedly move the muscles cause tears in muscle fibers, which grow back bigger. Lifting weights and gymnastics are forms of resistance training.

4 True or false: Women need more calories than men.
▲ False
On average, men need more calories than women as they are often bigger and have larger muscles.

5 What happens to the heart during exercise?
● Beats faster
When muscles work hard they need more oxygen, so the heart beats faster to supply the muscles with what they need.

6 **Which of these is not a type of aerobic exercise?**

● Weight lifting

Aerobic exercise is a continual movement, like cycling. Weight lifting is anaerobic, as it involves sudden bursts of movement.

7 **True or false: Brain cells work more effectively after exercise.**

◆ True

Exercise increases blood flow to the brain, and this helps it function.

8 **Why is it important to drink plenty of water when working out?**

● Lots of fluids are lost when sweating.

There is more risk of dehydration when sweating a lot, so it's vital to top up fluid levels by drinking enough water.

9 **During exercise, breathing increases from 15 times per minute to up to . . .**

● 60 times per minute

As the body works harder, it uses more oxygen and produces more carbon dioxide.

10 **Which activity will use up the most energy?**

■ Star jumping

All of these activities use up energy, but the more vigorous the exercise, the more energy the body needs to function.

Podium!

Bronze: 1–5 correct answers
Silver: 6–8 correct answers
Gold: 9–10 correct answers

Sweat

Try out this quiz all about sweat. Don't lose your cool, you've got this!

1 What are sweaty palms a sign of?
- ◆ Tiredness
- ▲ Nerves or anxiety
- ● Hunger
- ■ Strength

2 Which part of the skin contains sweat glands?
- ◆ Epidermis
- ▲ Dermis
- ● Detritus

3 What is the optimum body temperature?
- ◆ 93.2°F (34°C)
- ▲ 98.6°F (37°C)
- ● 104°F (40°C)

4 What is the name of the nervous system that controls the involuntary process of sweating?
- ◆ Autonomic nervous system
- ▲ Automatic nervous system
- ● Autopilot nervous system

5 True or false: Every hour, the body loses at least 3.5 pts (2 liters) of water.
- ◆ True
- ▲ False

6 Which part of the brain monitors the water in the blood?
- ◆ Hypothalamus
- ▲ Brain stem
- ● Frontal lobe

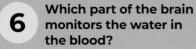

Did you know?

The amount that you urinate depends on how much you drink and sweat.

7 Put the process of sweating in the correct order:
- ◆ Moisture begins to form on the skin
- ▲ Body cools down
- ● The moisture evaporates
- ■ Body heats up from exercising

8 What is the purpose of sweating?
- ◆ To warm the body up
- ▲ To prove how hard you have worked
- ● To cool the body down

9 Which is not a way that the body loses water?
- ◆ By sweating
- ▲ By urinating
- ● By drinking a milkshake
- ■ By going for a poo

10 Can humans last for longer without food or water?
- ◆ Food
- ▲ Water
- ● Neither—we need both equally

Turn to page 84 for the answers!

Sweat Answers

1 **What are sweaty palms a sign of?**

▲ Nerves or anxiety

Sweat pores in the palms of the hand open and make them damp.

2 **Which part of the skin contains sweat glands?**

▲ Dermis

The thick lower layer of the skin is the dermis. It contains sweat glands that release watery sweat onto the skin's surface.

3 **What is the optimum body temperature?**

▲ 98.6°F (37°C)

Warmer or colder temperatures disrupt the balance of the body, so wearing cooler or warmer clothing helps the body to cope.

4 **What is the name of the nervous system that controls the involuntary process of sweating?**

◆ Autonomic nervous system

As well as deliberate processes, such as walking, the nervous system also controls the beat of the heart, breathing, and tear glands.

5 True or false: Every hour, the body loses at least 3.5 pts (2 liters) of water.

▲ False

The body loses this amount of water each day.

6 Which part of the brain monitors the water in the blood?

◆ Hypothalamus

If water levels in the body are low, the hypothalamus triggers the sense of thirst to encourage the person to drink.

7 Put the process of sweating in the correct order:

■ Body heats up from exercising

◆ Moisture begins to form on the skin

● The moisture evaporates

▲ Body cools down

8 What is the purpose of sweating?

● To cool the body down

Sweating helps the body to regulate its temperature and prevent overheating.

9 Which is not a way that the body loses water?

● By drinking a milkshake

A milkshake may not be water, but it is a liquid and it will help to keep the body hydrated.

10 Can humans last for longer without food or water?

◆ Food

Without a regular supply of water to replace the moisture the body is constantly losing through sweating, a person can become ill.

Podium!

Bronze: 1–5 correct answers

Silver: 6–8 correct answers

Gold: 9–10 correct answers

Blood

Find out if all your learning about the human body has been in vain . . .

1 Which system transports blood around your body?
- ◆ Digestive
- ▲ Endocrine
- ● Cardiovascular

2 True or false: Veins carry blood away from the heart while arteries take blood toward it.
- ◆ True
- ▲ False

3 What is the name of the largest artery in the human body?
- ◆ Porta
- ▲ Aorta
- ● Chorta

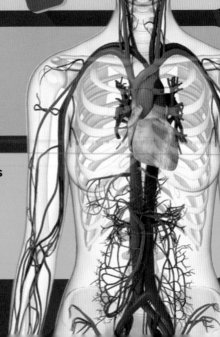

4 How many main blood groups are there?
- ◆ Two
- ▲ Four
- ● Six

5 True or false: Blood contains five types of blood cell.
- ◆ True
- ▲ False

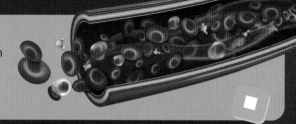

Did you know?
There are 5 million red blood cells in each drop of human blood.

6 How fast does the heart pump blood through the aorta?
◆ 1 mph (1.6 kph)
▲ 10 mph (16 kph)
● 100 mph (160 kph)

7 What is the name of the circuit that links the heart and the lungs?
◆ Systemic circuit
▲ Pulmonary circuit
● Arterial circuit

8 Your pulse can be taken from which artery in the wrist?
◆ Radial artery
▲ Diametrical artery
● Subclavian artery

9 Where do renal veins carry blood from and to?
◆ Brain to lungs
▲ Kidneys to heart
● Heart to liver

10 True or false: Caterpillars are the smallest blood vessels
◆ True
▲ False

Scan the QR code for a Kahoot! about blood.

Turn to page 88 for the answers!

Blood
Answers

1 **Which system transports blood around your body?**

● Cardiovascular

Also known as the circulatory system, this is the intricate network of arteries and veins in your body.

2 **True or false: Veins carry blood away from the heart while arteries take blood toward it.**

▲ False

Arteries carry blood away from the heart, and veins carry blood toward it.

3 **What is the name of the largest artery in the human body?**

▲ Aorta

Running from the heart to the pelvis, it is as thick as an adult's thumb.

4 **How many main blood groups are there?**

▲ Four

The groups are A, B, AB, and O. Type O can be donated to people of any blood group.

5 **True or false: Blood contains five types of blood cell.**

▲ False

It consists of three types of blood cell—red blood cells, white blood cells, and platelets—as well as a fluid called plasma.

6 How fast does the heart pump blood through the aorta?

◆ 1 mph (1.6 kph)

Each blood cell travels through the heart and around the body 1,000 times a day.

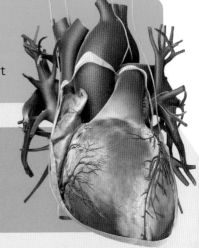

7 What is the name of the circuit that links the heart and the lungs?

▲ Pulmonary circuit

The word "pulmonary" comes from the Latin word for lungs—*pulmo*.

8 Your pulse can be taken from which artery in the wrist?

◆ Radial artery

If you press gently on the radial artery you can feel the blood pumping through your wrist. Arteries expand and spring back as blood travels through them.

9 Where do renal veins carry blood from and to?

▲ Kidneys to heart

The renal artery delivers blood to the kidneys, where the blood is cleaned. The blood then travels back to the heart through the renal vein.

10 True or false: Caterpillars are the smallest blood vessels

▲ False

The smallest blood vessels in the human body are capillaries. They are about one-tenth of the diameter of a human hair.

Podium!

Bronze: 1–5 correct answers
Silver: 6–8 correct answers
Gold: 9–10 correct answers

X-Rays

Do you understand the bare bones of these questions? This quiz will reveal all.

1 What was the first ever X-ray image?
- ◆ A woman's hand
- ▲ A dog's paw
- ● A man's foot
- ■ A cat's tail

2 When was the first X-ray taken?
- ◆ 1895
- ▲ 1899
- ● 1905

3 What are X-rays?
- ◆ Powerful waves of energy
- ▲ Strong beams of light
- ● Ultrasonic sound

4 True or false: X-rays project soundwaves through the body onto a photographic plate.
- ◆ True
- ▲ False

5 Why would a dentist take an X-ray of your teeth?
- ◆ To count your teeth
- ▲ To spot cavities
- ● To check your teeth have grown properly

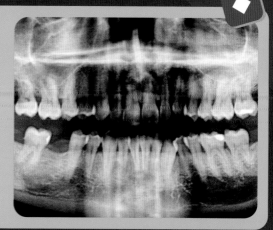

6 **What does the white part of an X-ray show?**
◆ Bones
▲ Muscles
● Organs

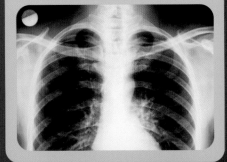

7 **X-rays are used for treatment too. What can they do?**
◆ Mend broken bones
▲ Fix holes in teeth
● Kill cancerous growths

Did you know?
X-rays were once used in shoe shops to examine how well the new shoes fitted each customer's feet.

8 **Why do only bones show up on an X-ray?**
◆ Because bones absorb the rays of radiation
▲ Because organs and muscles are invisible
● Because your blood hides the rest of your insides

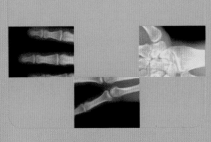

9 **What is an angiogram?**
◆ A type of X-ray where a dye is injected first, making parts other than bones visible
▲ An X-ray when the camera is angled in a different way
● A type of musical instrument

10 **What part of the body does this X-ray show?**
◆ The hand
▲ The foot
● The head

Turn to page 92 for the answers!

X-Rays Answers

1 **What was the first ever X-ray image?**

◆ A woman's hand

The first X-ray was of the hand of scientist Wilhelm Röntgen's wife.

2 **When was the first X-ray taken?**

◆ 1895

This changed diagnosis, treatments, and surgery for good!

3 **What are X-rays?**

◆ Powerful waves of energy

Like light, X-rays are a form of radiation. They are very useful because they can go through substances that light cannot.

4 **True or false: X-rays project soundwaves through the body onto a photographic plate.**

▲ False

X-rays use radiation projected through the body onto a photographic plate.

5 **Why would a dentist take an X-ray of your teeth?**

▲ To spot cavities

A dentist might use an X-ray to identify teeth that need to be filled.

6 What does the white part of an X-ray show?

◆ Bones

Bones are shown as white, and the soft parts (like muscles and organs) come up black.

7 X-rays are used for treatment too. What can they do?

● Kill cancerous growths

Radiotherapy uses high doses of radiation to shrink tumors.

8 Why do only bones show up on an X-ray?

◆ Because bones absorb the rays of radiation

Softer body tissues are not visible, as the X-rays pass right through them.

9 What is an angiogram?

◆ A type of X-ray where a dye is injected first, making parts other than bones visible

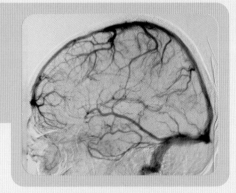

10 What part of the body does this X-ray show?

◆ The hand

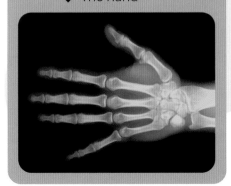

Podium!

Bronze: 1–5 correct answers

Silver: 6–8 correct answers

Gold: 9–10 correct answers

Touch

Make sure you don't lose your nerve with this quiz all about touch.

1 What organ is most linked to touch?
- ◆ Skin
- ▲ Heart
- ● Lungs

2 Nerve networks in the skin carry signals between touch receptors and the . . .
- ◆ Lungs
- ▲ Brain
- ● Heart

3 Which part of the face is super sensitive?
- ◆ Eyebrows
- ▲ Mouth
- ● Nose
- ■ Chin

4 What is the upper layer of the skin called?
- ◆ Gland
- ▲ Epidermis
- ● Dermis

5 True or false: The brain filters out less important messages from touch receptors.
- ◆ True
- ▲ False

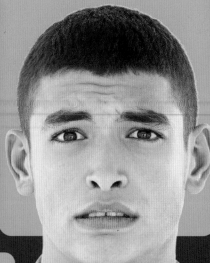

6 What do the most sensitive parts of the skin contain lots of?
- ◆ Hair
- ▲ Sense receptors
- ● Fatty tissue

7 What percentage of body weight is skin?
- ◆ 2 percent
- ▲ 5 percent
- ● 11 percent
- ■ 16 percent

8 Why is it important that lips are sensitive?
- ◆ To feel the texture of the teeth
- ▲ To help when applying make-up
- ● To stop people burning or harming their insides

Did you know?
The skin has different receptors to respond to heat, cold, or touch.

9 Which sensation can't we feel with touch?
- ◆ Texture
- ▲ Taste
- ● Pressure
- ■ Temperature

Scan the QR code for a Kahoot! about touch.

10 True or false: When in danger, the body has reflexes that mean they can move without engaging the brain.
- ◆ True
- ▲ False

Turn to page 96 for the answers!

Touch
Answers

1 **What organ is most linked to touch?**

◆ Skin

Skin is the first thing that comes into contact with the world around us.

2 **Nerve networks in the skin carry signals between touch receptors and the . . .**

▲ Brain

The sensory area of the brain processes sensations from touch organs.

3 **Which part of the face is super sensitive?**

▲ Mouth

The mouth is packed with touch receptors to quickly identify food and drink that's too hot or cold.

4 **What is the name of the upper layer of the skin?**

▲ Epidermis

New skin cells are created in the epidermis and replace old cells when they move to the surface of your skin.

5 **True or false: The brain filters out less important messages from touch receptors.**

◆ True

If the brain didn't filter it, our senses would be overloaded, and we would constantly feel every fiber next to our skin.

6
What do the most sensitive parts of the skin contain lots of?

▲ Sense receptors

The skin is packed with sense receptors to help identify whether something is hot or cold, sharp or smooth, and if it is wet or dry.

7
What percentage of body weight is skin?

■ 16 percent

Skin is the body's biggest organ and makes up about 16 percent of a person's overall body weight.

8
Why is it important that lips are sensitive?

● To stop people burning or harming their insides

Sensitive lips help identify substances before they enter the rest of the body.

9
Which sensation can't we feel with touch?

▲ Taste

There are no cells in the skin that detect taste—these are found mainly on the tongue and oral cavity.

10
True or false: When in danger, the body has reflexes that mean they can move without engaging the brain.

◆ True

Automatic reflexes protect the body, such as moving away from something that is too hot.

Podium!

Bronze: 1–5 correct answers
Silver: 6–8 correct answers
Gold: 9–10 correct answers

Liver

What do you know about this incredible organ? Here's hoping this quiz live(r)s up to your expectations!

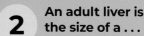

1 **Where in your body is the liver found?**
- ◆ In front of the lower ribs
- ▲ Behind the lower ribs
- ● Next to the intestines

2 **An adult liver is the size of a . . .**
- ◆ Grape
- ▲ Tennis ball
- ● A Soccer ball
- ■ Pea

3 **What does the liver secrete?**
- ◆ Bile
- ▲ Urine
- ● Sweat

4 **Which of these is not a job of the liver?**
- ◆ Remove toxins from the body
- ▲ Keep the body warm
- ● Maintain blood sugar levels
- ■ Regulate blood clotting

5 **What is a common sign of poor liver function?**
- ◆ Dry skin
- ▲ Jaundice
- ● Curly hair

6 Which system does the liver belong to?
◆ Respiration
▲ Digestion
● Reproduction

7 True or false: The liver is the largest organ within your body.
◆ True
▲ False

8 What acids are found in the liver during digestion?
◆ Amino acids
▲ Hydrochloric acid
● Fatty acids

Did you know?
The liver is able to regenerate lost or damaged tissue cells. It can regrow, even if up to 90 percent of it has been removed.

9 How much blood does the liver receive every minute?
◆ 1/2 pint (0.25 liters)
▲ 1 pint (0.5 liters)
● 2.5 pints (1.5 liters)

10 During digestion, the liver . . .
◆ Has a rest
▲ Processes nutrients
● Pumps oxygen around the body

Turn to page 100 for the answers!

Liver
Answers

1 **Where in your body is the liver found?**

▲ Behind the lower ribs

The liver is found in the upper right side of the body.

2 **An adult liver is the size of a . . .**

● A Soccer ball

It weighs up to 3 pounds—that's the same as three loaves of bread.

3 **What does the liver secrete?**

◆ Bile

Bile is a digestive fluid that is stored and released by the liver.

4 **Which of these is not a job of the liver?**

▲ Keep the body warm

The liver has lots of important jobs—especially filtering blood and removing toxins—but keeping us warm is not one of them.

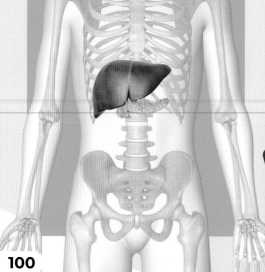

5 What is a common sign of poor liver function?

▲ Jaundice

When someone has jaundice, the white of their eyes and skin can yellow.

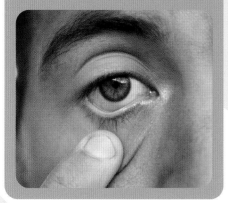

6 Which system does the liver belong to?

▲ Digestion

By producing bile, the liver prepares fats for the next stage in digestion and absorption.

7 True or false: The liver is the largest organ within your body.

◆ True

The liver is the biggest and heaviest organ inside your body. The skin is the biggest, but that's on the outside.

8 What acids are found in the liver during digestion?

◆ Amino acids

Amino acids are transported to the liver for protein production.

9 How much blood does the liver receive every minute?

● 2.5 pints (1.5 liters)

The hepatic artery is the name of the artery that takes blood to the liver.

10 During digestion, the liver . . .

▲ Processes nutrients

The liver processes and stores nutrients from the food before releasing them into the body to be used.

Podium!

Bronze: 1–5 correct answers
Silver: 6–8 correct answers
Gold: 9–10 correct answers

Stomach

Get ready to fill up with facts by testing your knowledge of the stomach.

1 What do stomach muscles do when food enters?
- ◆ Do a star jump
- ▲ Vibrate
- ● Contract and relax

2 What happens after the food is emptied from the stomach?
- ◆ The stomach stops moving altogether.
- ▲ The stomach muscles keep moving.
- ● The stomach goes to sleep.

3 True or false: Food can stay in the stomach for more than five hours.
- ◆ True
- ▲ False

4 Which part of the stomach releases digestive juices?
- ◆ Stomach lining
- ▲ Stomach muscles
- ● Gullet

5 To help break down food, the stomach produces . . .
- ◆ Bacteria
- ▲ Enzymes and acids
- ● Protein

6 Why does the stomach need protective mucus?

◆ Because it's scared of the dark

▲ Because the stomach acid is so strong

● Because it always catches colds

Did you know?

Food is churned up into a soup-like mixture in the stomach, known as "chyme."

7 The stomach is best described as which shape?

◆ Star

▲ Letter "J"

● Football

■ Letter "S"

8 Where does food go after it leaves the stomach?

◆ Lungs

▲ Small intestine

● Kidneys

9 How many layers of muscle are in the stomach wall?

◆ One

▲ Two

● Three

Scan the QR code for a Kahoot! about the stomach.

Turn to page 104 for the answers!

10 What part of the stomach produces acid to destroy germs in food?

◆ Stomach glands

▲ Stomach muscle

● Stomach mucus

Stomach
Answers

1 **What do stomach muscles do when food enters?**

● Contract and relax

This motion helps the stomach to mix up and break down food.

2 **What happens after the food is emptied from the stomach?**

▲ The stomach muscles keep moving.

This is the sensation of hunger.

3 **True or false: Food can stay in the stomach for more than five hours.**

◆ True

Food gets broken into smaller pieces in the stomach.

4 **Which part of the stomach releases digestive juices?**

◆ Stomach lining

Stomach muscles churn the food together, but it's the lining that produces the juices.

5 **To help break down food, the stomach produces . . .**

▲ Enzymes and acids

Enzymes split complex chemicals into substances the body can use.

6 Why does the stomach need protective mucus?

▲ Because the stomach acid is so strong

Without protective mucus, the stomach acid would mean the stomach would digest itself.

7 The stomach is best described as which shape?

▲ Letter "J"

The stomach is a stretchy sack. It is attached to the esophagus and the duodenum, which is the first part of the small intestine.

8 Where does food go after it leaves the stomach?

▲ Small intestine

This is where most food is digested.

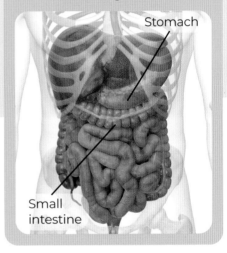

Stomach

Small intestine

9 How many layers of muscle are in the stomach wall?

● Three

Within the stomach wall, the three layers of muscle overlap in different directions.

10 What part of the stomach produces acid to destroy germs in food?

◆ Stomach glands

Found in the stomach wall, stomach glands produce a very powerful acid to kill germs from food and the mucus from the throat.

Podium!

Bronze: 1–5 correct answers
Silver: 6–8 correct answers
Gold: 9–10 correct answers

Intestines

Gut ready to journey into the intestines and test your knowledge!

1 If you stretched out the small intestine, how long would it be?
- ◆ As long as one adult
- ▲ As long as four adults laid head to toe
- ● As long as 10 adults laid head to toe

2 True or false: The large intestine is much shorter than the small intestine, but double the width.
- ◆ True
- ▲ False

3 What system is the small intestine and the large intestine part of?
- ◆ The nervous system
- ▲ The digestive system
- ● The cardiovascular system

4 What does the muscle in the intestines do?
- ◆ Squeeze and relax in a wavelike motion
- ▲ Let everything slide through
- ● Squeeze tightly shut until told to relax

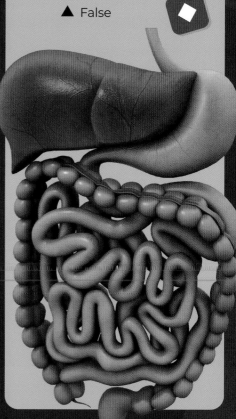

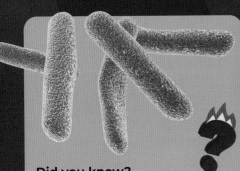

Did you know?
Bacteria in the large intestine produce a number of different vitamins, especially vitamin K and biotin, a B vitamin.

5 What does the large intestine turn the waste that comes from the small intestine into?
◆ Blood
▲ Sweat
● Feces

6 What is the picture of?
◆ Villi
▲ Rugae

7 How long is the lifespan of the cells in the small intestine?
◆ 4 days
▲ 6 hours
● 36 hours

8 How many bacteria live in the large intestine?
◆ Millions
▲ Billions
● Trillions

9 Where does most of the digestive process take place?
◆ The small intestine
▲ The large intestine

10 What is the first part of the small intestine called?
◆ Duodenum
▲ Jejunum
● Ileum

Turn to page 108 for the answers!

Intestines
Answers

1 If you stretched out the small intestine, how long would it be?

▲ As long as four adults laid head to toe

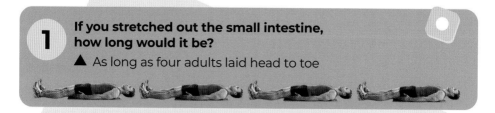

2 True or false: The large intestine is much shorter than the small intestine, but double the width.

◆ True

The large intestine is a quarter of the length of the small intestine.

3 What system is the small intestine and the large intestine part of?

▲ The digestive system

The digestive tract runs from the mouth to the anus. It includes the esophagus and the stomach.

4 What does the muscle in the intestines do?

◆ Squeeze and relax in a wavelike motion

This process both mixes food and moves it onward.

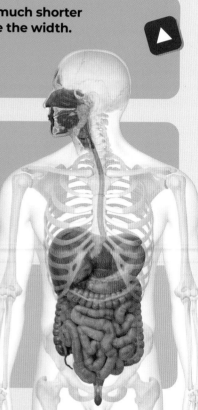

5 What does the large intestine turn the waste that comes from the small intestine into?

● Feces

The large intestine absorbs water from the waste, and feces are formed as the water is removed.

6 What is the picture of?

◆ Villi

Microscopic villi line the small intestine and provide a surface for absorption and digestion. Rugae, however, are deep folds in the stomach wall that disappear when it stretches, as it fills with food.

7 How long is the lifespan of the cells in the small intestine?

● 36 hours

Cells don't all last the same time—brain cells may last a lifetime!

8 How many bacteria live in the large intestine?

● Trillions

Most of the bacteria are harmless or helpful, and help process any nutrients that haven't been broken down by enzymes.

9 Where does most of the digestive process take place?

◆ The small intestine

The small intestine releases the nutrients in food so they can be used to fuel the body's cells.

Podium!

Bronze: 1–5 correct answers
Silver: 6–8 correct answers
Gold: 9–10 correct answers

10 What is the first part of the small intestine called?

◆ Duodenum

This is where the bile and enzymes are added to help break everything down.

Kidneys

Are you kidney-ing me?
You're ready for even
more questions?

1 **What do kidneys make?**
- ◆ Urine
- ▲ Blood
- ● Water

2 **What carries blood out of the kidneys?**
- ◆ Renal vein
- ▲ Renal artery
- ● Adrenal gland

3 **Your kidneys make up 1 percent of your weight, but how much oxygen do they use?**
- ◆ 10 percent
- ▲ 15 percent
- ● 25 percent

4 **True or false: In an average lifetime, the kidneys process 79 million pints (45 million liters) of blood.**
- ◆ True
- ▲ False

Did you know?

Your kidneys don't just filter and clean blood to make urine. They help to control your blood pressure to make sure it stays within safe limits. Blood pressure is the measure of the force your heart pumps blood around your body.

5 How long do your kidneys take to clean your entire blood supply?
◆ Less than an hour
▲ A whole day
● 24 hours

6 Put the process of the urinary system in order:
◆ The urine is pushed to the bladder.
▲ Urine flows out of the body in the urethra.
● The kidneys produce urine.
■ Urine is stored in the bladder.

7 Where do the kidneys sit?
◆ Behind the stomach and either side of the spine
▲ Above the lungs
● Under the lower intestine

8 Which of these things do your kidneys not do?
◆ Filter blood and remove toxins
▲ Break down food
● Stimulate red blood cell production
■ Keep the body's water supply balanced

9 Can you live with just one kidney?
◆ Yes
▲ No

10 What shape are your kidneys?
◆ Mushroom shaped
▲ Bean shaped
● Apple shaped

Scan the QR code for a Kahoot! about kidneys.

Turn to page 112 for the answers!

Kidneys
Answers

1 **What do your kidneys make?**

◆ Urine

Kidneys make urine from liquid waste and extra water from your blood.

2 **What carries blood out of the kidneys?**

◆ Renal vein

The renal artery carries the blood in to be cleaned. The adrenal gland releases adrenaline.

3 **Your kidneys make up 1 percent of your weight, but how much oxygen do they use?**

● 25 percent

They also release a hormone that increases the production of red blood cells in your body.

4 **True or false: In an average lifetime, the kidneys process 79 million pints (45 million liters) of blood.**

◆ True

It's enough to fill 18 Olympic-size swimming pools.

5 **How long do your kidneys take to clean your entire blood supply?**

◆ Less than an hour

Your body cleans and filters about 2 pints (1 liter) a minute!

6 Put the process of the urinary system in order:

- ● The kidneys produce urine.
- ◆ The urine is pushed to the bladder.
- ■ Urine is stored in the bladder.
- ▲ Urine flows out of the body in the urethra.

7 Where do the kidneys sit?

- ◆ Behind the stomach and either side of the spine

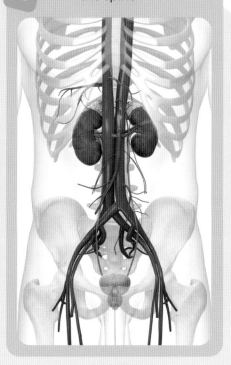

8 Which of these things do your kidneys not do?

- ▲ Break down food

Acid and enzymes found in the stomach breaks down food.

9 Can you live with just one kidney?

- ◆ Yes

But if someone has damaged or diseased kidneys, a dialysis machine can be used to filter the blood instead.

10 What shape are your kidneys?

- ▲ Bean shaped

Kidney beans are so named because of their similarity in shape and color to human kidneys.

Podium!

Bronze: 1–5 correct answers

Silver: 6–8 correct answers

Gold: 9–10 correct answers

Growth

Where did you grow?
Come back and do this
quiz right now!

1 How does something grow?
◆ Cells multiply and divide
▲ Cells get bigger
and bigger

Did you know?
Growth doesn't just
happen. The size and form
of plants and animals are
controlled by genes.

2 What chemical controls
the speed your body
grows during childhood
and teenage years?
◆ Growth hormone
▲ Speed hormone
● Height hormone

3 The growth hormone
is made by specialized
cells in which gland?
◆ Adrenal gland
▲ Pituitary gland
● Thyroid gland

4 Growth hormones
make every organ in
the body grow bigger
apart from the . . .
◆ Liver
▲ Brain
● Skin

5 Which system does the growth hormone boost?
◆ Immune system
▲ Endocrine system
● Nervous system

6 True or false: This X-ray shows an adult hand.
◆ True
▲ False

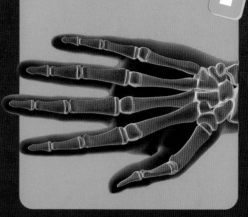

7 What hormone does the liver release when told to by the growth hormone?
◆ 2GF-1
▲ 3GF-1
● IGF-1

8 A fetus begins as one single cell. Nine months later, how many cells does the newborn baby's body consist of?
◆ About 5 billion cells
▲ About 2 trillion cells
● About 3 trillion cells

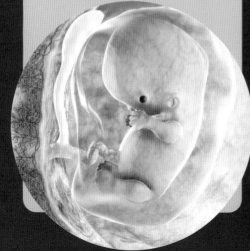

9 If someone has a lack of growth hormone, what can happen?
◆ A condition called dwarfism
▲ A condition called gigantism

10 Growing isn't always just getting bigger. If cells are damaged what happens?
◆ Regeneration
▲ Regrowth
● Rewire

Turn to page 116 for the answers!

Growth
Answers

1 **How does something grow?**
◆ Cells multiply and divide
Growth takes place when cells increase in size and number.

2 **What chemical controls the speed your body grows during childhood and teenage years?**
◆ Growth hormone
It affects every part of the body. It makes organs larger, muscles stronger, and bones longer.

3 **The growth hormone is made by specialized cells in which gland?**
▲ Pituitary gland
The pituitary gland is found in your brain. It produces hormones that control other glands in the body.

4 **Growth hormones make every organ in the body grow bigger, apart from the . . .**
▲ Brain
The brain is the most complex organ in the entire living world.

5 **Which system does the growth hormone boost?**
◆ Immune system
Research has shown that future treatments could use the growth hormone to help with immune deficiencies.

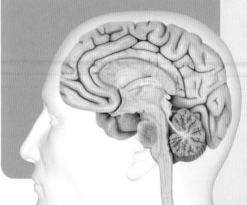

6 **True or false: This X-ray shows an adult hand.**

◆ True

A child's hand has gaps at the growth plates where the long bones are still growing. In an adult's hand the growth plates have filled with bone.

7 **What hormone does the liver release when told to by the growth hormone?**

● IGF-1

It causes bones to grow longer and wider.

8 **A fetus begins as one single cell. Nine months later, how many cells does the newborn baby's body consist of?**

● About 3 trillion cells

At week five, it's the size of an apple seed. At week 10, it's the size of an olive!

9 **If someone has a lack of growth hormone, what can happen?**

◆ A condition called dwarfism

This is when someone is shorter than usual, and it is caused by an underactive pituitary gland. Gigantism, however, is a condition when someone grows more than usual, and is caused by an overactive pituitary gland.

10 **Growing isn't always just getting bigger. If cells are damaged, what happens?**

◆ Regeneration

Often the new growth does not look like the original, but it performs the role it is supposed to. For example, when a deep cut on human skin closes with new skin growth, it may leave a scar.

Podium!

Bronze: 1–5 correct answers
Silver: 6–8 correct answers
Gold: 9–10 correct answers

Sleeping

ZZZ! Let's get dreaming . . .
I mean quizzing! Just don't
fall asleep halfway through!

1 **How much of our lives do we spend sleeping?**
- ◆ A third
- ▲ A half
- ● A quarter

2 **Can you put these five different stages of sleep in order?**
- ◆ Delta brain waves first appear
- ▲ Drowsy, light sleep
- ● REM sleep
- ■ Deep sleep for about 30 minutes

3 **True or false: Sleepwalkers have been known to cook meals, drive cars, and even send emails, though they have no memory of doing so later.**
- ◆ True
- ▲ False

4 **What is the part of the brain that controls sleeping?**
- ◆ Hypothalamus
- ▲ Hippocampus
- ● Cerebellum

5 **If you're at school, how much sleep do you need?**
- ◆ Between 8 and 10 hours
- ▲ Between 10 and 12 hours
- ● Between 12 and 14 hours

6 Which of these brain waves occur when you're in a deep sleep?
- ◆ Alpha
- ▲ Beta
- ● Delta
- ■ Theta

7 What does REM stand for?
- ◆ Rich eye mash
- ▲ Rapid eye movement
- ● Root eye master

Did you know?

In 1964, American student Randy Gardner broke a world record by going 11 days without sleeping.

8 When do you first start to dream?
- ◆ From the age of three years
- ▲ When you're still in your mother's womb
- ● From when you're born

9 What does sleep not do?
- ◆ Help our genes behave
- ▲ Teach us a new language
- ● Help our body clock regulate itself
- ■ Keep us healthy

Scan the QR code for a Kahoot! about sleeping.

Turn to page 120 for the answers!

10 Which age group needs the most sleep?
- ◆ Children
- ▲ Teenagers
- ● Adults

Sleeping

Answers

1 How much of our lives do we spend sleeping?

◆ A third

We can't live without sleep!

2 Can you put these five different stages of sleep in order?

▲ Drowsy, light sleep

◆ Delta brain waves first appear

■ Deep sleep for about 30 minutes

● REM sleep

3 True or false: Sleepwalkers have been known to cook meals, drive cars, and even send emails, though they have no memory of doing so later.

◆ True

Sleepwalking takes place during deep sleep and is not connected with dreams.

4 What is the part of the brain that controls sleeping?

◆ Hypothalamus

It sends signals to many other parts of the brain and body to control activity.

5 If you're at school, how much sleep do you need?

◆ Between 8 and 10 hours

School children need between 8 and 10 hours of sleep each day. Babies need as much as 16 hours a day to develop normally. Adults can manage on only 7 hours.

6 Which of these brain waves occur when you're in a deep sleep?

● Delta

Delta waves happen when you're in deep sleep, during stages 3 and 4. Alpha waves occur when you're awake but relaxed. Beta waves are produced when you're alert. Theta waves come when you are drowsy.

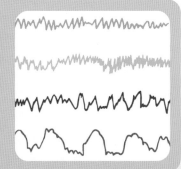

7 What does REM stand for?

▲ Rapid eye movement

REM occurs when we are asleep and our brains are highly active.

8 When do you first start to dream?

▲ When you're still in your mother's womb

Roughly 20 weeks before a baby is born, it starts to dream.

9 What does sleep not do?

▲ Teach us a new language

Our genes can behave differently when we don't get enough sleep. We think better if we've had enough sleep. Not sleeping well can also disturb our immune system.

10 Which age group needs the most sleep?

▲ Teenagers

Teenagers need the most sleep, as their sleeping hormones are released late at night, making waking up harder.

Podium!

Bronze: 1–5 correct answers
Silver: 6–8 correct answers
Gold: 9–10 correct answers

Technology

From prosthetic limbs to bionic bots, how much do you know about medical advances?

1 What is the name of the testing carried out to check for inherited illnesses?
- ◆ Driving tests
- ▲ Genetic testing
- ● Software testing

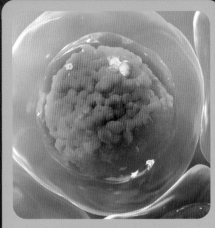

2 Which type of cells can be implanted into people to repair damaged cells?
- ◆ Stetson cells
- ▲ Steam cells
- ● Stem cells

3 How many new stem cells does the body produce every day?
- ◆ 300 million
- ▲ 300 billion
- ● 300 trillion

4 True or false: Synthetic skin allows people to feel objects with more sensitivity than with human limbs.
- ◆ True
- ▲ False

5 What were the first known prosthetic body parts?

◆ Toes
▲ Legs
● Arms

6 When would a bionic suit be helpful?

◆ For moon walking
▲ Rehabilitating someone to walk again after an injury
● To be in two places at once

7 What historical event led to artificial limbs being produced on a mass scale?

◆ Sinking of the Titanic
▲ World War I
● World War II

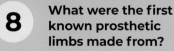

Did you know?

In the future, scientists hope to develop mini nanobots that they can inject into the bloodstream to destroy bacteria.

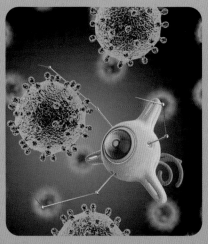

8 What were the first known prosthetic limbs made from?

◆ Bone and cartilage
▲ Plastic
● Wood and leather

9 What do scientists hope to use to tackle the shortage of organs suitable for transplants?

◆ 3D printing
▲ Knitting
● Sewing

Turn to page 124 for the answers!

Technology
Answers

1 What is the name of the testing carried out to check for inherited illnesses?

▲ Genetic testing

This testing is life-saving, as it can help predict possible illnesses before they happen.

2 Which type of cells can be implanted into people to repair damaged cells?

● Stem cells

Scientists can manipulate stem cells to develop in particular ways to treat specific illnesses.

3 How many new stem cells does the body produce every day?

▲ 300 billion

Stem cells are always dividing. There are about 200 cell types, all with different jobs to do.

4 True or false: Synthetic skin allows people to feel objects with more sensitivity than with human limbs.

▲ False

Advances in synthetic skin mean it can be as sensitive as human skin, but not more so.

5 What were the first known prosthetic body parts?

◆ Toes

Artificial toes were discovered dating back to Ancient Egypt.
Big toes are believed to carry 40 percent of the body's weight.

6 When would a bionic suit be helpful?

▲ Rehabilitating someone to walk again after an injury

These exoskeletons can help give people the strength to walk again after using a wheelchair.

7 What historical event led to artificial limbs being produced on a mass scale?

▲ World War I

The large number of casualties meant there was a huge demand for prosthetic limbs for war veterans.

8 What were the first known prosthetic limbs made from?

● Wood and leather

Today, prosthetic limbs are constantly advancing and are made using much lighter, more durable, and flexible materials.

9 What do scientists hope to use to tackle the shortage of organs suitable for transplants?

◆ 3D printing

Researchers would make a scan of the existing organ, and use this to program the printer and build a new organ.

Podium!

Bronze: 1–4 correct answers

Silver: 5–7 correct answers

Gold: 8–9 correct answers

Glossary

Antibody

A protective protein that is part of the immune system, and produced in response to toxins or antigens in the body.

Collagen

The main protein produced by the body that is found in the skin and other tissues providing structure.

Dermis

Thick middle layer of living tissue found below the epidermis layer. It protects your body and produces sweat and hair.

Endocrine system

A messenger system that involves tissue that produces and releases hormones that travel in the bloodstream to control other organs or cells.

Endoscopy

An instrument is introduced into the body in order to view its internal parts.

Enzyme

A protein that creates and speeds up chemical reactions within a living cell to help support life.

Gustatory system

The system in the body relating to eating, and the perception of taste.

Olfactory system

The system involving the nose and nasal cavities that forms someone's sense of smell.

Papillae

Small bumps on the top of the tongue that contain taste buds and help grip food.

Pulmonary circuit

The system of blood vessels connecting the heart and lungs, involving the oxygenation of blood.

Radioactive

Something that emits radiation by producing powerful and dangerous energy as a result of the breaking up of atoms.

Retina

Layer at the back of the eyeball containing light-sensitive cells that receive images and send them as electric signals to the brain.

Picture Credits

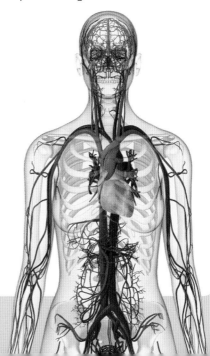

The publisher would like to thank the following for their kind permission to reproduce their photographs:

(Key: a-above; b-below/bottom; c-centre; f-far; l-left; r-right; t-top)

2 Dreamstime.com: Sebastian Kaulitzki (bl). **3 123RF.com:** Antonio Guillem (tr). **Dreamstime. com:** Paul-andr Belle-isle (br); Thorsten Nilson (bl). **5 Dreamstime.com:** Igor Zakharevich (cra). **6 Dorling Kindersley:** Arran Lewis / Zygote (r). **9 Dreamstime.com:** Gordana Sermek (tr). **Fotolia:** Natallia Yaumenenka / eAlisa (cr). **10 Dreamstime.com:** Myeteck (cr); Parkinsonsniper (br). **11 Dreamstime.com:** Pongsak Deethongngam (crb). **Getty Images / iStock:** Onandter_sean (cla). **14 Dreamstime.com:** Thorsten Nilson (br). **15 Dreamstime.com:** Stockyimages (cla). **17 Dorling Kindersley:** Arran Lewis / Zygote (clb). **Dreamstime.com:** Thorsten Nilson (cr). **18 Dreamstime.com:** Pongmoji (cr); Rixie (br). **19 Dreamstime.com:** Ermilovart83 (tl). **20 123RF.com:** Antonio Guillem (bl). **21 Dreamstime.com:** Ramona Smiers (cr). **26 Dreamstime.com:** Margoe Edwards (cra). **Getty Images / iStock:** ScantyNebula (cl). **27 Dreamstime.com:** Paul Hakimata (bl). **Fotolia:** billyhoiler (cra). **28 Dreamstime.com:** Roman Samborskyi (br). **30 Dreamstime.com:** Paul Hakimata (br). **35 Dreamstime.com:** Vadymvdrobot (cra). **40 Dreamstime.com:** Deyangeorgiev (tr). **41 Getty Images:** Penelope Grasshoff / EyeEm (cr). **42 Dreamstime.com:** Stangot (br). **43 Dreamstime.com:** Andreykuzmin (cb); Sathit Plengchawee (tr). **44 Dreamstime.com:** Yulianny (bl). **45 Dreamstime. com:** Andreykuzmin (cr); Yvdavyd (cla). **49 123RF. com:** Richard Thomas (tl). **50 Dreamstime.com:** Stuartbur (br). **Getty Images:** Photographer's Choice RF / Jon Boyes (br/Plate). **51 Dreamstime. com:** Markus Gann / Magann (tr); Monkey Business Images (cl). **53 Dreamstime.com:** Piksel (clb). **56 Dreamstime.com:** Hughstoneian (br). **59 Dreamstime.com:** Sam74100 (cl). **PunchStock:** Image Source (tr). **60 Dreamstime.com:** Rattanachot2525 (cl). **61 123RF.com:** jovannig (tl). **62 Dreamstime.com:** Fizkes (bl); Alexandr Mitiuc (crb). **64 Dreamstime.com:** Antonio Guillem (bl). **67 Dreamstime.com:** Piotr Marcinski (tl). **70 Dreamstime.com:** Paul-andr Belle-isle (cl); Taskinceyhan (crb). **73 Getty Images:** Nicholas Eveleigh / Photodisc (cl). **74 Fotolia:** Fotoedgaras (br). **75 Dreamstime.com:** Erikreis (cl); Kts (tr). **77 123RF.com:** pockygallery (clb). **79 123RF.com:** ocusfocus (cla). **Dreamstime.com:** Akulamatiau (tr). **80 123RF.com:** Todd Arena (crb). **82 Dreamstime.com:** BY (bl); Korn Vitthayanukarun (cra). **83 Dreamstime.com:** Meinzahn (cr); Alexey Prokopyev (ca). **87 Dreamstime.com:** Igor Zakharevich (tr). **90 Dreamstime.com:** Saaaaa (br). **91 Dreamstime.com:** Itsmejust (clb); Radub85 (cla). **92 Dreamstime.com:** Nerthuz (cr). **93 Dreamstime.com:** Itsmejust (bl); Vesna Njagulj (cr). **94 Dreamstime.com:** Srckomkrit (cr). **95 Dreamstime.com:** Valentyn75 (c); Xxlphoto (cra). **96 Dreamstime.com:** Makidotvn (br). **101 Dreamstime.com:** Creative Cat Studio (cla). **104 Dreamstime.com:** Sebastian Kaulitzki / Eraxion (br). **106 Dreamstime.com:** Brijith Vijayan (br). **107 Dreamstime.com:** Sebastian Kaulitzki (cr); Andrey Sukhachev / Nchuprin (tl). **110 Getty Images:** Nicholas Eveleigh / Photodisc (bc). **111 Dreamstime.com:** Unlim3d (clb). **112 Dreamstime.com:** Erinpackardphotography (br). **114 Dreamstime.com:** Sebastian Kaulitzki (cra). **115 Dorling Kindersley:** Zygote (cra). **122 Dreamstime.com:** Ironjohn (cl); Siarhei Yurchanka (cr). **123 Dreamstime.com:** Ken Backer (tr); Volodymyr Horbovyy (bl). **124 Dreamstime. com:** Ivan Soto (br). **125 Dreamstime.com:** Chaiyon021 (tr); Svteam (cl). **126 Dreamstime. com:** Unlim3d (br). **127 Fotolia:** billyhoiler (cra). **128 Dreamstime.com:** Andrey Sukhachev / Nchuprin (clb); Brijith Vijayan (cla)

Cover images: *Front:* **Dreamstime.com:** Skypixel cb; *Back:* **Fotolia:** billyhoiler tr

All other images © Dorling Kindersley

Dorling Kindersley would like to thank Morten Versvik, Ritesh Maisuria, Perla P. Pinto, Francisco Bembibre, and Craig Narveson at Kahoot!
DK also thanks David McDonald, James McKeag, and Isabelle Merry for design assistance, Bipasha Choudhury for fact checking, and Victoria Taylor for proofreading.

DK | Penguin Random House

Senior Art Editor Anna Formanek
Cover design James McKeag and Isabelle Merry
US Editors Susan Hobbs and Lori Hand
Senior Production Editor Jennifer Murray
Senior Production Controller Lloyd Robertson
Managing Editor Paula Regan
Managing Art Editor Jo Connor
Publishing Director Mark Searle

Packaged for DK by Dynamo Limited

First American Edition, 2023
Published in the United States by DK Publishing
1745 Broadway, 20th Floor,
New York, NY 10019

Page design copyright © 2023 Dorling Kindersley Limited
DK, a Division of Penguin Random House LLC
23 24 25 26 27 10 9 8 7 6 5 4 3 2 1
001–334340–Sept/2023

A CIP catalog record for this book
is available from the Library of Congress.
ISBN: 978-0-7440-7661-5

Printed and bound in China

For the curious
www.dk.com
www.kahoot.com

create.kahoot.it/profiles/dk-learning-us